ISO IEC 27001 Lead Implementer Complete Self-Assessment Guide

C000100818

The guidance in this Self-Assessment is ba
Lead Implementer best practices and stan
architecture, design and quality management. The guidance is also based
on the professional judgment of the individual collaborators listed in the
Acknowledgments.

Notice of rights

Trademarks

Table of Contents

About The Art of Service

The Art of Service, Business Process Architects since 2000, is dedicated to helping stakeholders achieve excellence.

Defining, designing, creating, and implementing a process to solve a stakeholders challenge or meet an objective is the most valuable role… In EVERY group, company, organization and department.

Unless you're talking a one-time, single-use project, there should be a process. Whether that process is managed and implemented by humans, AI, or a combination of the two, it needs to be designed by someone with a complex enough perspective to ask the right questions.

Someone capable of asking the right questions and step back and say, 'What are we really trying to accomplish here? And is there a different way to look at it?'

With The Art of Service's Standard Requirements Self-Assessments, we empower people who can do just that — whether their title is marketer, entrepreneur, manager, salesperson, consultant, Business Process Manager, executive assistant, IT Manager, CIO etc… —they are the people who rule the future. They are people who watch the process as it happens, and ask the right questions to make the process work better.

Contact us when you need any support with this Self-Assessment and any help with templates, blue-prints and examples of standard documents you might need:

http://theartofservice.com
service@theartofservice.com

Acknowledgments

This checklist was developed under the auspices of The Art of Service, chaired by Gerardus Blokdyk.

Representatives from several client companies participated in the preparation of this Self-Assessment.

Our deepest gratitude goes out to Matt Champagne, Ph.D. Surveys Expert, for his invaluable help and advise in structuring the Self Assessment.

In addition, we are thankful for the design and printing services provided.

Included Resources - how to access

Included with your purchase of the book is the ISO IEC 27001 Lead Implementer Self-Assessment Spreadsheet Dashboard which contains all questions and Self-Assessment areas and auto-generates insights, graphs, and project RACI planning - all with examples to get you started right away.

How? Simply send an email to
access@theartofservice.com
with this books' title in the subject to get the ISO IEC 27001 Lead Implementer Self Assessment Tool right away.

You will receive the following contents with New and Updated specific criteria:
* The latest quick edition of the book in PDF
* The latest complete edition of the book in PDF, which criteria correspond to the criteria in...
* The Self-Assessment Excel Dashboard, and...
* Example pre-filled Self-Assessment Excel Dashboard to get familiar with results generation
* ...plus an extra, special, resource that helps you with project

managing.

INCLUDES LIFETIME SELF ASSESSMENT UPDATES

Every self assessment comes with Lifetime Updates and Lifetime Free Updated Books. Lifetime Updates is an industry-first feature which allows you to receive verified self assessment updates, ensuring you always have the most accurate information at your fingertips.

Get it now- you will be glad you did - do it now, before you forget.

Send an email to **access@theartofservice.com** with this books' title in the subject to get the ISO IEC 27001 Lead Implementer Self Assessment Tool right away.

Your feedback is invaluable to us

If you recently bought this book, we would love to hear from you! You can do this by writing a review on amazon (or the online store where you purchased this book) about your last purchase! As part of our continual service improvement process, we love to hear real client experiences and feedback.

How does it work?
To post a review on Amazon, just log in to your account and click on the Create Your Own Review button (under Customer Reviews) of the relevant product page. You can find examples of product reviews in Amazon. If you purchased from another online store, simply follow their procedures.

What happens when I submit my review?
Once you have submitted your review, send us an email at review@theartofservice.com with the link to your review so we can properly thank you for your feedback.

Purpose of this Self-Assessment

This Self-Assessment has been developed to improve understanding of the requirements and elements of ISO IEC 27001 Lead Implementer, based on best practices and standards in business process architecture, design and quality management.

It is designed to allow for a rapid Self-Assessment to determine how closely existing management practices and procedures correspond to the elements of the Self-Assessment.

The criteria of requirements and elements of ISO IEC 27001 Lead Implementer have been rephrased in the format of a Self-Assessment questionnaire, with a seven-criterion scoring system, as explained in this document.

In this format, even with limited background knowledge of ISO IEC

27001 Lead Implementer, a manager can quickly review existing operations to determine how they measure up to the standards. This in turn can serve as the starting point of a 'gap analysis' to identify management tools or system elements that might usefully be implemented in the organization to help improve overall performance.

How to use the Self-Assessment

On the following pages are a series of questions to identify to what extent your ISO IEC 27001 Lead Implementer initiative is complete in comparison to the requirements set in standards.

To facilitate answering the questions, there is a space in front of each question to enter a score on a scale of '1' to '5'.

1 Strongly Disagree

2 Disagree

3 Neutral

4 Agree

5 Strongly Agree

Read the question and rate it with the following in front of mind:

'In my belief, the answer to this question is clearly defined'.

There are two ways in which you can choose to interpret this statement;
1. how aware are you that the answer to the question is clearly defined
2. for more in-depth analysis you can choose to gather

evidence and confirm the answer to the question. This obviously will take more time, most Self-Assessment users opt for the first way to interpret the question and dig deeper later on based on the outcome of the overall Self-Assessment.

A score of '1' would mean that the answer is not clear at all, where a '5' would mean the answer is crystal clear and defined. Leave emtpy when the question is not applicable or you don't want to answer it, you can skip it without affecting your score. Write your score in the space provided.

After you have responded to all the appropriate statements in each section, compute your average score for that section, using the formula provided, and round to the nearest tenth. Then transfer to the corresponding spoke in the ISO IEC 27001 Lead Implementer Scorecard on the second next page of the Self-Assessment.

Your completed ISO IEC 27001 Lead Implementer Scorecard will give you a clear presentation of which ISO IEC 27001 Lead Implementer areas need attention.

ISO IEC 27001 Lead Implementer Scorecard Example

Example of how the finalized Scorecard can look like:

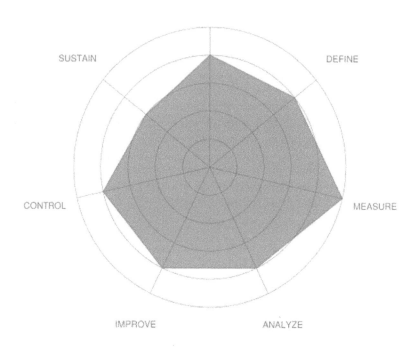

ISO IEC 27001 Lead Implementer Scorecard

Your Scores:

BEGINNING OF THE SELF-ASSESSMENT:

CRITERION #1: RECOGNIZE

INTENT: Be aware of the need for change. Recognize that there is an unfavorable variation, problem or symptom.

In my belief, the answer to this question is clearly defined:

5 Strongly Agree

4 Agree

3 Neutral

2 Disagree

1 Strongly Disagree

1. What training and capacity building actions are needed to implement proposed reforms?
<--- Score

2. Who needs to know about ISO IEC 27001 Lead Implementer ?
<--- Score

3. How much are sponsors, customers, partners,

stakeholders involved in ISO IEC 27001 Lead Implementer? In other words, what are the risks, if ISO IEC 27001 Lead Implementer does not deliver successfully?

<--- Score

4. For your ISO IEC 27001 Lead Implementer project, identify and describe the business environment. is there more than one layer to the business environment?

<--- Score

5. What do we need to start doing?

<--- Score

6. As a sponsor, customer or management, how important is it to meet goals, objectives?

<--- Score

7. What would happen if ISO IEC 27001 Lead Implementer weren't done?

<--- Score

8. Will a response program recognize when a crisis occurs and provide some level of response?

<--- Score

9. Who defines the rules in relation to any given issue?

<--- Score

10. How do you identify the information basis for later specification of performance or acceptance criteria?

<--- Score

11. Does our organization need more ISO IEC

27001 Lead Implementer education?

<--- Score

12. Who else hopes to benefit from it?

<--- Score

13. Can Management personnel recognize the monetary benefit of ISO IEC 27001 Lead Implementer?

<--- Score

14. How are the ISO IEC 27001 Lead Implementer's objectives aligned to the organization's overall business strategy?

<--- Score

15. Why do we need to keep records?

<--- Score

16. What situation(s) led to this ISO IEC 27001 Lead Implementer Self Assessment?

<--- Score

17. What should be considered when identifying available resources, constraints, and deadlines?

<--- Score

18. What is the smallest subset of the problem we can usefully solve?

<--- Score

19. Think about the people you identified for your ISO IEC 27001 Lead Implementer project and the project responsibilities you would assign to them. what kind of training do you think they would need to perform these responsibilities effectively?

<--- Score

20. What does ISO IEC 27001 Lead Implementer success mean to the stakeholders?

<--- Score

21. Will it solve real problems?

<--- Score

22. Are there recognized ISO IEC 27001 Lead Implementer problems?

<--- Score

23. Will ISO IEC 27001 Lead Implementer deliverables need to be tested and, if so, by whom?

<--- Score

24. How do we Identify specific ISO IEC 27001 Lead Implementer investment and emerging trends?

<--- Score

25. What vendors make products that address the ISO IEC 27001 Lead Implementer needs?

<--- Score

26. Are controls defined to recognize and contain problems?

<--- Score

27. Are there any specific expectations or concerns about the ISO IEC 27001 Lead Implementer team, ISO IEC 27001 Lead Implementer itself?

<--- Score

28. What problems are you facing and how do you consider ISO IEC 27001 Lead Implementer will circumvent those obstacles?

<--- Score

29. Will new equipment/products be required to facilitate ISO IEC 27001 Lead Implementer delivery for example is new software needed?
<--- Score

30. Does ISO IEC 27001 Lead Implementer create potential expectations in other areas that need to be recognized and considered?
<--- Score

31. How does it fit into our organizational needs and tasks?
<--- Score

32. Consider your own ISO IEC 27001 Lead Implementer project. what types of organizational problems do you think might be causing or affecting your problem, based on the work done so far?
<--- Score

33. Do we know what we need to know about this topic?
<--- Score

34. Have you identified your ISO IEC 27001 Lead Implementer key performance indicators?
<--- Score

35. What are the expected benefits of ISO IEC 27001 Lead Implementer to the business?
<--- Score

36. Who had the original idea?

<--- Score

37. What prevents me from making the changes I know will make me a more effective ISO IEC 27001 Lead Implementer leader?

<--- Score

38. How do you identify the kinds of information that you will need?

<--- Score

39. What are the business objectives to be achieved with ISO IEC 27001 Lead Implementer?

<--- Score

40. When a ISO IEC 27001 Lead Implementer manager recognizes a problem, what options are available?

<--- Score

41. Cloud management for ISO IEC 27001 Lead Implementer do we really need one?

<--- Score

42. Is it clear when you think of the day ahead of you what activities and tasks you need to complete?

<--- Score

43. How do you assess your ISO IEC 27001 Lead Implementer workforce capability and capacity needs, including skills, competencies, and staffing levels?

<--- Score

44. How can auditing be a preventative security

measure?
<--- Score

45. What else needs to be measured?
<--- Score

46. Are there ISO IEC 27001 Lead Implementer problems defined?
<--- Score

47. How are we going to measure success?
<--- Score

48. What tools and technologies are needed for a custom ISO IEC 27001 Lead Implementer project?
<--- Score

49. What information do users need?
<--- Score

Add up total points for this section:
_ _ _ _ _ = Total points for this section

Divided by: _ _ _ _ _ _ (number of statements answered) = _ _ _ _ _ _
Average score for this section

Transfer your score to the ISO IEC 27001 Lead Implementer Index at the beginning of the Self-Assessment.

CRITERION #2: DEFINE:

INTENT: Formulate the business problem. Define the problem, needs and objectives.

In my belief, the answer to this question is clearly defined:

5 Strongly Agree

4 Agree

3 Neutral

2 Disagree

1 Strongly Disagree

1. What tools and roadmaps did you use for getting through the Define phase?
<--- Score

2. Is full participation by members in regularly held team meetings guaranteed?
<--- Score

3. Is it clearly defined in and to your organization what

you do?
<--- Score

4. In what way can we redefine the criteria of choice clients have in our category in our favor?
<--- Score

5. What are the Roles and Responsibilities for each team member and its leadership? Where is this documented?
<--- Score

6. How often are the team meetings?
<--- Score

7. Is there a completed, verified, and validated high-level 'as is' (not 'should be' or 'could be') business process map?
<--- Score

8. What is the minimum educational requirement for potential new hires?
<--- Score

9. How and when will the baselines be defined?
<--- Score

10. Are different versions of process maps needed to account for the different types of inputs?
<--- Score

11. How will variation in the actual durations of each activity be dealt with to ensure that the expected ISO IEC 27001 Lead Implementer results are met?
<--- Score

12. Is there a completed SIPOC representation, describing the Suppliers, Inputs, Process, Outputs, and Customers?
<--- Score

13. What key business process output measure(s) does ISO IEC 27001 Lead Implementer leverage and how?
<--- Score

14. Has a project plan, Gantt chart, or similar been developed/completed?
<--- Score

15. Is there regularly 100% attendance at the team meetings? If not, have appointed substitutes attended to preserve cross-functionality and full representation?
<--- Score

16. Is the team equipped with available and reliable resources?
<--- Score

17. When was the ISO IEC 27001 Lead Implementer start date?
<--- Score

18. What are the compelling business reasons for embarking on ISO IEC 27001 Lead Implementer?
<--- Score

19. Are approval levels defined for contracts and supplements to contracts?
<--- Score

20. How would one define ISO IEC 27001 Lead

Implementer leadership?
<--- Score

21. Are task requirements clearly defined?
<--- Score

22. Are there any constraints known that bear on the ability to perform ISO IEC 27001 Lead Implementer work? How is the team addressing them?
<--- Score

23. What customer feedback methods were used to solicit their input?
<--- Score

24. Has everyone on the team, including the team leaders, been properly trained?
<--- Score

25. Is ISO IEC 27001 Lead Implementer Required?
<--- Score

26. Is there a critical path to deliver ISO IEC 27001 Lead Implementer results?
<--- Score

27. Do we all define ISO IEC 27001 Lead Implementer in the same way?
<--- Score

28. Do the problem and goal statements meet the SMART criteria (specific, measurable, attainable, relevant, and time-bound)?
<--- Score

29. Are audit criteria, scope, frequency and methods

defined?

<--- Score

30. Does the team have regular meetings?

<--- Score

31. How is the team tracking and documenting its work?

<--- Score

32. What constraints exist that might impact the team?

<--- Score

33. Is the current 'as is' process being followed? If not, what are the discrepancies?

<--- Score

34. How does the ISO IEC 27001 Lead Implementer manager ensure against scope creep?

<--- Score

35. Is a fully trained team formed, supported, and committed to work on the ISO IEC 27001 Lead Implementer improvements?

<--- Score

36. What are the dynamics of the communication plan?

<--- Score

37. Is there a ISO IEC 27001 Lead Implementer management charter, including business case, problem and goal statements, scope, milestones, roles and responsibilities, communication plan?

<--- Score

38. Are customer(s) identified and segmented according to their different needs and requirements?
<--- Score

39. Has anyone else (internal or external to the organization) attempted to solve this problem or a similar one before? If so, what knowledge can be leveraged from these previous efforts?
<--- Score

40. Has the improvement team collected the 'voice of the customer' (obtained feedback – qualitative and quantitative)?
<--- Score

41. Are accountability and ownership for ISO IEC 27001 Lead Implementer clearly defined?
<--- Score

42. How will the ISO IEC 27001 Lead Implementer team and the organization measure complete success of ISO IEC 27001 Lead Implementer?
<--- Score

43. Are customers identified and high impact areas defined?
<--- Score

44. In what way can we redefine the criteria of choice in our category in our favor, as Method introduced style and design to cleaning and Virgin America returned glamor to flying?
<--- Score

45. Have all basic functions of ISO IEC 27001 Lead

Implementer been defined?
<--- Score

46. What defines Best in Class?
<--- Score

47. What are the boundaries of the scope? What is in bounds and what is not? What is the start point? What is the stop point?
<--- Score

48. Is the improvement team aware of the different versions of a process: what they think it is vs. what it actually is vs. what it should be vs. what it could be?
<--- Score

49. What baselines are required to be defined and managed?
<--- Score

50. How would you define the culture here?
<--- Score

51. Has the direction changed at all during the course of ISO IEC 27001 Lead Implementer? If so, when did it change and why?
<--- Score

52. Is the ISO IEC 27001 Lead Implementer scope manageable?
<--- Score

53. Who defines (or who defined) the rules and roles?
<--- Score

54. How was the 'as is' process map developed,

reviewed, verified and validated?
<--- Score

55. Will team members regularly document their ISO IEC 27001 Lead Implementer work?
<--- Score

56. What would be the goal or target for a ISO IEC 27001 Lead Implementer's improvement team?
<--- Score

57. Have the customer needs been translated into specific, measurable requirements? How?
<--- Score

58. Are improvement team members fully trained on ISO IEC 27001 Lead Implementer?
<--- Score

59. How do you keep key subject matter experts in the loop?
<--- Score

60. Have all of the relationships been defined properly?
<--- Score

61. How did the ISO IEC 27001 Lead Implementer manager receive input to the development of a ISO IEC 27001 Lead Implementer improvement plan and the estimated completion dates/times of each activity?
<--- Score

62. When is the estimated completion date?
<--- Score

63. Are team charters developed?
<--- Score

64. How can the value of ISO IEC 27001 Lead Implementer be defined?
<--- Score

65. Is the team formed and are team leaders (Coaches and Management Leads) assigned?
<--- Score

66. Is the team adequately staffed with the desired cross-functionality? If not, what additional resources are available to the team?
<--- Score

67. Are business processes mapped?
<--- Score

68. Are Required Metrics Defined?
<--- Score

69. What specifically is the problem? Where does it occur? When does it occur? What is its extent?
<--- Score

70. Are there different segments of customers?
<--- Score

71. Has the ISO IEC 27001 Lead Implementer work been fairly and/or equitably divided and delegated among team members who are qualified and capable to perform the work? Has everyone contributed?
<--- Score

72. What critical content must be communicated – who, what, when, where, and how?
<--- Score

73. When are meeting minutes sent out? Who is on the distribution list?
<--- Score

74. Is the scope of ISO IEC 27001 Lead Implementer defined?
<--- Score

75. Who are the ISO IEC 27001 Lead Implementer improvement team members, including Management Leads and Coaches?
<--- Score

76. Have specific policy objectives been defined?
<--- Score

77. Is ISO IEC 27001 Lead Implementer linked to key business goals and objectives?
<--- Score

78. Is the team sponsored by a champion or business leader?
<--- Score

79. Will team members perform ISO IEC 27001 Lead Implementer work when assigned and in a timely fashion?
<--- Score

80. Is ISO IEC 27001 Lead Implementer currently on schedule according to the plan?
<--- Score

81. Has/have the customer(s) been identified?
<--- Score

82. Has a team charter been developed and communicated?
<--- Score

83. Are roles and responsibilities formally defined?
<--- Score

84. Are security/privacy roles and responsibilities formally defined?
<--- Score

85. What are the rough order estimates on cost savings/opportunities that ISO IEC 27001 Lead Implementer brings?
<--- Score

86. Has a high-level 'as is' process map been completed, verified and validated?
<--- Score

87. Is data collected and displayed to better understand customer(s) critical needs and requirements.
<--- Score

88. If substitutes have been appointed, have they been briefed on the ISO IEC 27001 Lead Implementer goals and received regular communications as to the progress to date?
<--- Score

Add up total points for this section:

_ _ _ _ _ = Total points for this section

Divided by: _ _ _ _ _ _ (number of statements answered) = _ _ _ _ _ _
Average score for this section

Transfer your score to the ISO IEC 27001 Lead Implementer Index at the beginning of the Self-Assessment.

CRITERION #3: MEASURE:

INTENT: Gather the correct data. Measure the current performance and evolution of the situation.

In my belief, the answer to this question is clearly defined:

5 Strongly Agree

4 Agree

3 Neutral

2 Disagree

1 Strongly Disagree

1. How is the value delivered by ISO IEC 27001 Lead Implementer being measured?
<--- Score

2. Are key measures identified and agreed upon?
<--- Score

3. Are there measurements based on task performance?

<--- Score

4. Which customers cant participate in our ISO IEC 27001 Lead Implementer domain because they lack skills, wealth, or convenient access to existing solutions?
<--- Score

5. Why Measure?
<--- Score

6. How will effects be measured?
<--- Score

7. Is long term and short term variability accounted for?
<--- Score

8. What measurements are being captured?
<--- Score

9. What Relevant Entities could be measured?
<--- Score

10. What evidence is there and what is measured?
<--- Score

11. Why do measure/indicators matter?
<--- Score

12. Do we aggressively reward and promote the people who have the biggest impact on creating excellent ISO IEC 27001 Lead Implementer services/products?
<--- Score

13. What about ISO IEC 27001 Lead Implementer Analysis of results?
<--- Score

14. Have all non-recommended alternatives been analyzed in sufficient detail?
<--- Score

15. How will your organization measure success?
<--- Score

16. Have you found any 'ground fruit' or 'low-hanging fruit' for immediate remedies to the gap in performance?
<--- Score

17. Does the ISO IEC 27001 Lead Implementer task fit the client's priorities?
<--- Score

18. Is this an issue for analysis or intuition?
<--- Score

19. What is measured?
<--- Score

20. What are your key ISO IEC 27001 Lead Implementer organizational performance measures, including key short and longer-term financial measures?
<--- Score

21. Are we taking our company in the direction of better and revenue or cheaper and cost?
<--- Score

22. How are measurements made?
<--- Score

23. Customer Measures: How Do Customers See Us?
<--- Score

24. Are the measurements objective?
<--- Score

25. Is a solid data collection plan established that includes measurement systems analysis?
<--- Score

26. Is there a Performance Baseline?
<--- Score

27. Was a data collection plan established?
<--- Score

28. What to measure and why?
<--- Score

29. Is key measure data collection planned and executed, process variation displayed and communicated and performance baselined?
<--- Score

30. What are our key indicators that you will measure, analyze and track?
<--- Score

31. What charts has the team used to display the components of variation in the process?
<--- Score

32. Is data collected on key measures that were

identified?
<--- Score

33. How is progress measured?
<--- Score

34. Will ISO IEC 27001 Lead Implementer have an impact on current business continuity, disaster recovery processes and/or infrastructure?
<--- Score

35. How can we measure the performance?
<--- Score

36. Have changes been properly/adequately analyzed for effect?
<--- Score

37. Are you taking your company in the direction of better and revenue or cheaper and cost?
<--- Score

38. How to measure lifecycle phases?
<--- Score

39. How do your measurements capture actionable ISO IEC 27001 Lead Implementer information for use in exceeding your customers expectations and securing your customers engagement?
<--- Score

40. Have the types of risks that may impact ISO IEC 27001 Lead Implementer been identified and analyzed?
<--- Score

41. What are the types and number of measures to use?
<--- Score

42. Schedule Development, Feasibility Analysis, ISO IEC 27001 Lead Implementer Management, Project Closings, Technique: Using the Critical Path Method
<--- Score

43. Which Stakeholder Characteristics Are Analyzed?
<--- Score

44. Have the concerns of stakeholders to help identify and define potential barriers been obtained and analyzed?
<--- Score

45. How do you measure success?
<--- Score

46. How are you going to measure success?
<--- Score

47. Is Process Variation Displayed/Communicated?
<--- Score

48. What data was collected (past, present, future/ongoing)?
<--- Score

49. Does ISO IEC 27001 Lead Implementer analysis show the relationships among important ISO IEC 27001 Lead Implementer factors?
<--- Score

50. How will measures be used to manage and adapt?

<--- Score

51. Does the practice systematically track and analyze outcomes related for accountability and quality improvement?
<--- Score

52. Among the ISO IEC 27001 Lead Implementer product and service cost to be estimated, which is considered hardest to estimate?
<--- Score

53. Who should receive measurement reports ?
<--- Score

54. Meeting the challenge: are missed ISO IEC 27001 Lead Implementer opportunities costing us money?
<--- Score

55. What methods are feasible and acceptable to estimate the impact of reforms?
<--- Score

56. What key measures identified indicate the performance of the business process?
<--- Score

57. What is the right balance of time and resources between investigation, analysis, and discussion and dissemination?
<--- Score

58. What are the costs of reform?
<--- Score

59. What measurements are possible, practicable and meaningful?
<--- Score

60. What are my customers expectations and measures?
<--- Score

61. What is an unallowable cost?
<--- Score

62. Where is it measured?
<--- Score

63. How is Knowledge Management Measured?
<--- Score

64. How to measure variability?
<--- Score

65. Is the solution cost-effective?
<--- Score

66. How frequently do we track measures?
<--- Score

67. Does ISO IEC 27001 Lead Implementer systematically track and analyze outcomes for accountability and quality improvement?
<--- Score

68. Can We Measure the Return on Analysis?
<--- Score

69. Why identify and analyze stakeholders and their interests?

<--- Score

70. Can we do ISO IEC 27001 Lead Implementer without complex (expensive) analysis?
<--- Score

71. Are process variation components displayed/ communicated using suitable charts, graphs, plots?
<--- Score

72. Why should we expend time and effort to implement measurement?
<--- Score

73. What will be measured?
<--- Score

74. Is data collection planned and executed?
<--- Score

75. Does ISO IEC 27001 Lead Implementer analysis isolate the fundamental causes of problems?
<--- Score

76. Are high impact defects defined and identified in the business process?
<--- Score

77. How will you measure your ISO IEC 27001 Lead Implementer effectiveness?
<--- Score

78. Do we effectively measure and reward individual and team performance?
<--- Score

79. When is Knowledge Management Measured?
<--- Score

80. Who participated in the data collection for measurements?
<--- Score

81. What are measures?
<--- Score

82. How do you identify and analyze stakeholders and their interests?
<--- Score

83. What are the agreed upon definitions of the high impact areas, defect(s), unit(s), and opportunities that will figure into the process capability metrics?
<--- Score

84. Are the units of measure consistent?
<--- Score

85. What is the total cost related to deploying ISO IEC 27001 Lead Implementer, including any consulting or professional services?
<--- Score

86. The approach of traditional ISO IEC 27001 Lead Implementer works for detail complexity but is focused on a systematic approach rather than an understanding of the nature of systems themselves. what approach will permit us to deal with the kind of unpredictable emergent behaviors that dynamic complexity can introduce?
<--- Score

87. How will success or failure be measured?
<--- Score

88. What are the key input variables? What are the key process variables? What are the key output variables?
<--- Score

89. How do we do risk analysis of rare, cascading, catastrophic events?
<--- Score

90. How do we focus on what is right -not who is right?
<--- Score

91. Is it possible to estimate the impact of unanticipated complexity such as wrong or failed assumptions, feedback, etc. on proposed reforms?
<--- Score

92. How large is the gap between current performance and the customer-specified (goal) performance?
<--- Score

93. Why do the measurements/indicators matter?
<--- Score

94. Will We Aggregate Measures across Priorities?
<--- Score

95. Are there any easy-to-implement alternatives to ISO IEC 27001 Lead Implementer? Sometimes other solutions are available that do not require the cost implications of a full-blown project?
<--- Score

96. Are losses documented, analyzed, and remedial processes developed to prevent future losses?
<--- Score

97. How frequently do you track ISO IEC 27001 Lead Implementer measures?
<--- Score

98. What should be measured?
<--- Score

99. Is performance measured?
<--- Score

100. How can you measure ISO IEC 27001 Lead Implementer in a systematic way?
<--- Score

101. What particular quality tools did the team find helpful in establishing measurements?
<--- Score

102. What has the team done to assure the stability and accuracy of the measurement process?
<--- Score

103. How Will We Measure Success?
<--- Score

104. Which customers can't participate in our market because they lack skills, wealth, or convenient access to existing solutions?
<--- Score

105. What are the uncertainties surrounding

estimates of impact?
<--- Score

106. What potential environmental factors impact the ISO IEC 27001 Lead Implementer effort?
<--- Score

107. Do staff have the necessary skills to collect, analyze, and report data?
<--- Score

Add up total points for this section:
_ _ _ _ _ = Total points for this section

Divided by: _ _ _ _ _ _ (number of statements answered) = _ _ _ _ _ _
Average score for this section

Transfer your score to the ISO IEC 27001 Lead Implementer Index at the beginning of the Self-Assessment.

CRITERION #4: ANALYZE:

INTENT: Analyze causes, assumptions and hypotheses.

In my belief, the answer to this question is clearly defined:

5 Strongly Agree

4 Agree

3 Neutral

2 Disagree

1 Strongly Disagree

1. Do our leaders quickly bounce back from setbacks?
<--- Score

2. Is the suppliers process defined and controlled?
<--- Score

3. What other jobs or tasks affect the performance of the steps in the ISO IEC 27001 Lead Implementer process?

<--- Score

4. How do you measure the Operational performance of your key work systems and processes, including productivity, cycle time, and other appropriate measures of process effectiveness, efficiency, and innovation?
<--- Score

5. An organizationally feasible system request is one that considers the mission, goals and objectives of the organization. key questions are: is the solution request practical and will it solve a problem or take advantage of an opportunity to achieve company goals?
<--- Score

6. Think about the functions involved in your ISO IEC 27001 Lead Implementer project. what processes flow from these functions?
<--- Score

7. What are our ISO IEC 27001 Lead Implementer Processes?
<--- Score

8. Teaches and consults on quality process improvement, project management, and accelerated ISO IEC 27001 Lead Implementer techniques
<--- Score

9. Is the suppliers process defined and controlled?
<--- Score

10. How was the detailed process map generated, verified, and validated?

<--- Score

11. Did any additional data need to be collected?
<--- Score

12. What were the crucial 'moments of truth' on the process map?
<--- Score

13. Where is the data coming from to measure compliance?
<--- Score

14. Have the problem and goal statements been updated to reflect the additional knowledge gained from the analyze phase?
<--- Score

15. What are the disruptive ISO IEC 27001 Lead Implementer technologies that enable our organization to radically change our business processes?
<--- Score

16. How often will data be collected for measures?
<--- Score

17. How do mission and objectives affect the ISO IEC 27001 Lead Implementer processes of our organization?
<--- Score

18. Were there any improvement opportunities identified from the process analysis?
<--- Score

19. A compounding model resolution with available relevant data can often provide insight towards a solution methodology; which ISO IEC 27001 Lead Implementer models, tools and techniques are necessary?

<--- Score

20. Think about some of the processes you undertake within your organization. which do you own?

<--- Score

21. What are the revised rough estimates of the financial savings/opportunity for ISO IEC 27001 Lead Implementer improvements?

<--- Score

22. Is Data and process analysis, root cause analysis and quantifying the gap/opportunity in place?

<--- Score

23. What does the data say about the performance of the business process?

<--- Score

24. What successful thing are we doing today that may be blinding us to new growth opportunities?

<--- Score

25. Do your employees have the opportunity to do what they do best everyday?

<--- Score

26. What are your current levels and trends in key measures or indicators of ISO IEC 27001 Lead Implementer product and process performance

that are important to and directly serve your customers? how do these results compare with the performance of your competitors and other organizations with similar offerings?
<--- Score

27. What are the best opportunities for value improvement?
<--- Score

28. Is the performance gap determined?
<--- Score

29. What tools were used to narrow the list of possible causes?
<--- Score

30. Is the ISO IEC 27001 Lead Implementer process severely broken such that a re-design is necessary?
<--- Score

31. What controls do we have in place to protect data?
<--- Score

32. Is the gap/opportunity displayed and communicated in financial terms?
<--- Score

33. What process should we select for improvement?
<--- Score

34. How does the organization define, manage, and improve its ISO IEC 27001 Lead Implementer processes?
<--- Score

35. Are gaps between current performance and the goal performance identified?
<--- Score

36. Have any additional benefits been identified that will result from closing all or most of the gaps?
<--- Score

37. Can we add value to the current ISO IEC 27001 Lead Implementer decision-making process (largely qualitative) by incorporating uncertainty modeling (more quantitative)?
<--- Score

38. How do you use ISO IEC 27001 Lead Implementer data and information to support organizational decision making and innovation?
<--- Score

39. How is the way you as the leader think and process information affecting your organizational culture?
<--- Score

40. Was a detailed process map created to amplify critical steps of the 'as is' business process?
<--- Score

41. What quality tools were used to get through the analyze phase?
<--- Score

42. What is the cost of poor quality as supported by the team's analysis?
<--- Score

43. What tools were used to generate the list of

possible causes?
<--- Score

44. What did the team gain from developing a sub-process map?
<--- Score

45. When conducting a business process reengineering study, what should we look for when trying to identify business processes to change?
<--- Score

46. Was a cause-and-effect diagram used to explore the different types of causes (or sources of variation)?
<--- Score

47. How do we promote understanding that opportunity for improvement is not criticism of the status quo, or the people who created the status quo?
<--- Score

48. Did any value-added analysis or 'lean thinking' take place to identify some of the gaps shown on the 'as is' process map?
<--- Score

49. Were Pareto charts (or similar) used to portray the 'heavy hitters' (or key sources of variation)?
<--- Score

50. Do you, as a leader, bounce back quickly from setbacks?
<--- Score

51. What other organizational variables, such as reward systems or communication systems, affect the performance of this ISO IEC 27001 Lead Implementer process?

<--- Score

52. Were any designed experiments used to generate additional insight into the data analysis?

<--- Score

53. Record-keeping requirements flow from the records needed as inputs, outputs, controls and for transformation of a ISO IEC 27001 Lead Implementer process. ask yourself: are the records needed as inputs to the ISO IEC 27001 Lead Implementer process available?

<--- Score

54. What were the financial benefits resulting from any 'ground fruit or low-hanging fruit' (quick fixes)?

<--- Score

55. What conclusions were drawn from the team's data collection and analysis? How did the team reach these conclusions?

<--- Score

56. Identify an operational issue in your organization. for example, could a particular task be done more quickly or more efficiently?

<--- Score

Add up total points for this section:
_ _ _ _ _ = Total points for this section

Divided by: _ _ _ _ _ _ (number of

statements answered) = _____
Average score for this section

Transfer your score to the ISO IEC
27001 Lead Implementer Index at the
beginning of the Self-Assessment.

CRITERION #5: IMPROVE:

INTENT: Develop a practical solution. Innovate, establish and test the solution and to measure the results.

In my belief, the answer to this question is clearly defined:

5 Strongly Agree

4 Agree

3 Neutral

2 Disagree

1 Strongly Disagree

1. Was a pilot designed for the proposed solution(s)?
<--- Score

2. Is there a small-scale pilot for proposed improvement(s)? What conclusions were drawn from the outcomes of a pilot?
<--- Score

3. Is the solution technically practical?

<--- Score

4. What should a proof of concept or pilot accomplish?
<--- Score

5. What is the implementation plan?
<--- Score

6. Are there any constraints (technical, political, cultural, or otherwise) that would inhibit certain solutions?
<--- Score

7. Is the optimal solution selected based on testing and analysis?
<--- Score

8. What lessons, if any, from a pilot were incorporated into the design of the full-scale solution?
<--- Score

9. Are we using ISO IEC 27001 Lead Implementer to communicate information about our Cybersecurity Risk Management programs including the effectiveness of those programs to stakeholders, including boards, investors, auditors, and insurers?
<--- Score

10. In the past few months, what is the smallest change we have made that has had the biggest positive result? What was it about that small change that produced the large return?
<--- Score

11. What is ISO IEC 27001 Lead Implementer's impact on utilizing the best solution(s)?
<--- Score

12. How did the team generate the list of possible solutions?
<--- Score

13. Why improve in the first place?
<--- Score

14. Is the measure understandable to a variety of people?
<--- Score

15. What is the magnitude of the improvements?
<--- Score

16. What tools were most useful during the improve phase?
<--- Score

17. What is the risk?
<--- Score

18. Do we cover the five essential competencies-Communication, Collaboration,Innovation, Adaptability, and Leadership that improve an organization's ability to leverage the new ISO IEC 27001 Lead Implementer in a volatile global economy?
<--- Score

19. If you could go back in time five years, what decision would you make differently? What is your best guess as to what decision you're making today

you might regret five years from now?
<--- Score

20. Risk events: what are the things that could go wrong?
<--- Score

21. What actually has to improve and by how much?
<--- Score

22. Is there a high likelihood that any recommendations will achieve their intended results?
<--- Score

23. What needs improvement?
<--- Score

24. How significant is the improvement in the eyes of the end user?
<--- Score

25. Are the best solutions selected?
<--- Score

26. Who controls the risk?
<--- Score

27. Is a solution implementation plan established, including schedule/work breakdown structure, resources, risk management plan, cost/budget, and control plan?
<--- Score

28. How do we Improve ISO IEC 27001 Lead Implementer service perception, and satisfaction?

<--- Score

29. What actually has to improve and by how much?

<--- Score

30. To what extent does management recognize ISO IEC 27001 Lead Implementer as a tool to increase the results?

<--- Score

31. What do we want to improve?

<--- Score

32. Are improved process ('should be') maps modified based on pilot data and analysis?

<--- Score

33. How will the team or the process owner(s) monitor the implementation plan to see that it is working as intended?

<--- Score

34. How do we improve productivity?

<--- Score

35. Are new and improved process ('should be') maps developed?

<--- Score

36. Explorations of the frontiers of ISO IEC 27001 Lead Implementer will help you build influence, improve ISO IEC 27001 Lead Implementer, optimize decision making, and sustain change

<--- Score

37. What error proofing will be done to address some of the discrepancies observed in the 'as is' process?
<--- Score

38. How important is the completion of a recognized college or graduate-level degree program in the hiring decision?
<--- Score

39. What are the implications of this decision 10 minutes, 10 months, and 10 years from now?
<--- Score

40. Who will be using the results of the measurement activities?
<--- Score

41. What is the team's contingency plan for potential problems occurring in implementation?
<--- Score

42. What improvements have been achieved?
<--- Score

43. How will we know that a change is improvement?
<--- Score

44. How do you manage and improve your ISO IEC 27001 Lead Implementer work systems to deliver customer value and achieve organizational success and sustainability?
<--- Score

45. How can we improve ISO IEC 27001 Lead Implementer?
<--- Score

46. How do we go about Comparing ISO IEC 27001 Lead Implementer approaches/solutions?
<--- Score

47. Is the implementation plan designed?
<--- Score

48. For decision problems, how do you develop a decision statement?
<--- Score

49. Is there a cost/benefit analysis of optimal solution(s)?
<--- Score

50. What can we do to improve?
<--- Score

51. Describe the design of the pilot and what tests were conducted, if any?
<--- Score

52. What attendant changes will need to be made to ensure that the solution is successful?
<--- Score

53. Can the solution be designed and implemented within an acceptable time period?
<--- Score

54. Who are the people involved in developing and implementing ISO IEC 27001 Lead Implementer?
<--- Score

55. How does the solution remove the key sources of

issues discovered in the analyze phase?

<--- Score

56. What tools do you use once you have decided on a ISO IEC 27001 Lead Implementer strategy and more importantly how do you choose?

<--- Score

57. Who will be responsible for documenting the ISO IEC 27001 Lead Implementer requirements in detail?

<--- Score

58. How Do We Link Measurement and Risk?

<--- Score

59. Is Supporting ISO IEC 27001 Lead Implementer documentation required?

<--- Score

60. Who controls key decisions that will be made?

<--- Score

61. How will the organization know that the solution worked?

<--- Score

62. What to do with the results or outcomes of measurements?

<--- Score

63. What were the underlying assumptions on the cost-benefit analysis?

<--- Score

64. How do you improve your likelihood of success ?

<--- Score

65. How do we measure improved ISO IEC 27001 Lead Implementer service perception, and satisfaction?

<--- Score

66. Is pilot data collected and analyzed?

<--- Score

67. What does the 'should be' process map/design look like?

<--- Score

68. What tools were used to tap into the creativity and encourage 'outside the box' thinking?

<--- Score

69. Does the goal represent a desired result that can be measured?

<--- Score

70. Do we combine technical expertise with business knowledge and ISO IEC 27001 Lead Implementer Key topics include lifecycles, development approaches, requirements and how to make a business case?

<--- Score

71. How can we improve performance?

<--- Score

72. How do we measure risk?

<--- Score

73. How do the ISO IEC 27001 Lead Implementer results compare with the performance of your competitors and other organizations with similar

offerings?
<--- Score

74. Is a contingency plan established?
<--- Score

75. Risk factors: what are the characteristics of ISO IEC 27001 Lead Implementer that make it risky?
<--- Score

76. How can skill-level changes improve ISO IEC 27001 Lead Implementer?
<--- Score

77. How to Improve?
<--- Score

78. How do we decide how much to remunerate an employee?
<--- Score

79. How do we keep improving ISO IEC 27001 Lead Implementer?
<--- Score

80. Who will be responsible for making the decisions to include or exclude requested changes once ISO IEC 27001 Lead Implementer is underway?
<--- Score

81. How do you measure progress and evaluate training effectiveness?
<--- Score

82. How does the team improve its work?
<--- Score

83. For estimation problems, how do you develop an estimation statement?

<--- Score

84. Are possible solutions generated and tested?

<--- Score

85. At what point will vulnerability assessments be performed once ISO IEC 27001 Lead Implementer is put into production (e.g., ongoing Risk Management after implementation)?

<--- Score

86. How will you know that you have improved?

<--- Score

87. What resources are required for the improvement effort?

<--- Score

88. Were any criteria developed to assist the team in testing and evaluating potential solutions?

<--- Score

89. What evaluation strategy is needed and what needs to be done to assure its implementation and use?

<--- Score

90. What communications are necessary to support the implementation of the solution?

<--- Score

91. What tools were used to evaluate the potential solutions?

<--- Score

92. Are we Assessing ISO IEC 27001 Lead Implementer
and Risk?
<--- Score

93. What went well, what should change, what can
improve?
<--- Score

94. How will you know when its improved?
<--- Score

95. How will you measure the results?
<--- Score

Add up total points for this section:
_ _ _ _ _ = Total points for this section

Divided by: _ _ _ _ _ _ (number of
statements answered) = _ _ _ _ _ _
Average score for this section

Transfer your score to the ISO IEC
27001 Lead Implementer Index at the
beginning of the Self-Assessment.

CRITERION #6: CONTROL:

INTENT: Implement the practical solution. Maintain the performance and correct possible complications.

In my belief, the answer to this question is clearly defined:

5 Strongly Agree

4 Agree

3 Neutral

2 Disagree

1 Strongly Disagree

1. How do we enable market innovation while controlling security and privacy?
<--- Score

2. Is there a control plan in place for sustaining improvements (short and long-term)?
<--- Score

3. Does ISO IEC 27001 Lead Implementer

appropriately measure and monitor risk?

<--- Score

4. Is there a recommended audit plan for routine surveillance inspections of ISO IEC 27001 Lead Implementer's gains?

<--- Score

5. Will existing staff require re-training, for example, to learn new business processes?

<--- Score

6. What key inputs and outputs are being measured on an ongoing basis?

<--- Score

7. How will input, process, and output variables be checked to detect for sub-optimal conditions?

<--- Score

8. What can you control?

<--- Score

9. Are operating procedures consistent?

<--- Score

10. Measure, Monitor and Predict ISO IEC 27001 Lead Implementer Activities to Optimize Operations and Profitably, and Enhance Outcomes

<--- Score

11. How will the process owner verify improvement in present and future sigma levels, process capabilities?

<--- Score

12. Strategic planning -ISO IEC 27001 Lead

Implementer relations
<--- Score

13. What other systems, operations, processes, and infrastructures (hiring practices, staffing, training, incentives/rewards, metrics/dashboards/scorecards, etc.) need updates, additions, changes, or deletions in order to facilitate knowledge transfer and improvements?
<--- Score

14. How do you encourage people to take control and responsibility?
<--- Score

15. How will the day-to-day responsibilities for monitoring and continual improvement be transferred from the improvement team to the process owner?
<--- Score

16. Were the planned controls in place?
<--- Score

17. What are the known security controls?
<--- Score

18. Is there a standardized process?
<--- Score

19. In the case of a ISO IEC 27001 Lead Implementer project, the criteria for the audit derive from implementation objectives. an audit of a ISO IEC 27001 Lead Implementer project involves assessing whether the recommendations outlined for implementation have been met. in

other words, can we track that any ISO IEC 27001 Lead Implementer project is implemented as planned, and is it working?

<--- Score

20. What is the recommended frequency of auditing?

<--- Score

21. Is there a ISO IEC 27001 Lead Implementer Communication plan covering who needs to get what information when?

<--- Score

22. What do we stand for--and what are we against?

<--- Score

23. What should the next improvement project be that is related to ISO IEC 27001 Lead Implementer?

<--- Score

24. Are controls in place and consistently applied?

<--- Score

25. What are your results for key measures or indicators of the accomplishment of your ISO IEC 27001 Lead Implementer strategy and action plans, including building and strengthening core competencies?

<--- Score

26. Whats the best design framework for ISO IEC 27001 Lead Implementer organization now that, in a post industrial-age if the top-down, command and control model is no longer relevant?

<--- Score

27. Can ISO IEC 27001 Lead Implementer be learned?
<--- Score

28. Who is the ISO IEC 27001 Lead Implementer
process owner?
<--- Score

29. What are we attempting to measure/monitor?
<--- Score

30. Does the ISO IEC 27001 Lead Implementer
performance meet the customer's requirements?
<--- Score

**31. How can we best use all of our knowledge
repositories to enhance learning and sharing?**
<--- Score

**32. Do you monitor the effectiveness of your ISO
IEC 27001 Lead Implementer activities?**
<--- Score

33. What should we measure to verify efficiency
gains?
<--- Score

34. Is there a transfer of ownership and knowledge
to process owner and process team tasked with the
responsibilities.
<--- Score

35. What quality tools were useful in the control
phase?
<--- Score

36. Have new or revised work instructions resulted?
<--- Score

37. Do the ISO IEC 27001 Lead Implementer decisions we make today help people and the planet tomorrow?
<--- Score

38. Does a troubleshooting guide exist or is it needed?
<--- Score

39. How will new or emerging customer needs/ requirements be checked/communicated to orient the process toward meeting the new specifications and continually reducing variation?
<--- Score

40. What are the key elements of your ISO IEC 27001 Lead Implementer performance improvement system, including your evaluation, organizational learning, and innovation processes?
<--- Score

41. What is the control/monitoring plan?
<--- Score

42. Who controls critical resources?
<--- Score

43. Are suggested corrective/restorative actions indicated on the response plan for known causes to problems that might surface?
<--- Score

44. Against what alternative is success being

measured?
<--- Score

45. Who has control over resources?
<--- Score

46. How do you select, collect, align, and integrate ISO IEC 27001 Lead Implementer data and information for tracking daily operations and overall organizational performance, including progress relative to strategic objectives and action plans?
<--- Score

47. What should we measure to verify effectiveness gains?
<--- Score

48. Is there a documented and implemented monitoring plan?
<--- Score

49. Is there documentation that will support the successful operation of the improvement?
<--- Score

50. How do our controls stack up?
<--- Score

51. ISO IEC 27001 Lead Implementer in management -Strategic planning
<--- Score

52. Where do ideas that reach policy makers and planners as proposals for ISO IEC 27001 Lead Implementer strengthening and reform actually

originate?
<--- Score

53. Are new process steps, standards, and documentation ingrained into normal operations?
<--- Score

54. How will report readings be checked to effectively monitor performance?
<--- Score

55. Is a response plan established and deployed?
<--- Score

56. Does job training on the documented procedures need to be part of the process team's education and training?
<--- Score

57. Were the planned controls working?
<--- Score

58. What is our theory of human motivation, and how does our compensation plan fit with that view?
<--- Score

59. Are pertinent alerts monitored, analyzed and distributed to appropriate personnel?
<--- Score

60. Is reporting being used or needed?
<--- Score

61. Has the improved process and its steps been standardized?

<--- Score

62. Is knowledge gained on process shared and institutionalized?
<--- Score

63. What is your theory of human motivation, and how does your compensation plan fit with that view?
<--- Score

64. What is your quality control system?
<--- Score

65. Does the response plan contain a definite closed loop continual improvement scheme (e.g., plan-do-check-act)?
<--- Score

66. How likely is the current ISO IEC 27001 Lead Implementer plan to come in on schedule or on budget?
<--- Score

67. Why is change control necessary?
<--- Score

68. How might the organization capture best practices and lessons learned so as to leverage improvements across the business?
<--- Score

69. Is new knowledge gained imbedded in the response plan?
<--- Score

70. What other areas of the organization might benefit

from the ISO IEC 27001 Lead Implementer team's improvements, knowledge, and learning?
<--- Score

71. Who will be in control?
<--- Score

72. Are there documented procedures?
<--- Score

73. Implementation Planning- is a pilot needed to test the changes before a full roll out occurs?
<--- Score

74. What are the critical parameters to watch?
<--- Score

75. Is a response plan in place for when the input, process, or output measures indicate an 'out-of-control' condition?
<--- Score

76. How do controls support value?
<--- Score

77. Will any special training be provided for results interpretation?
<--- Score

78. Are documented procedures clear and easy to follow for the operators?
<--- Score

79. How will the process owner and team be able to hold the gains?
<--- Score

80. Do the decisions we make today help people and the planet tomorrow?
<--- Score

81. Do we monitor the ISO IEC 27001 Lead Implementer decisions made and fine tune them as they evolve?
<--- Score

Add up total points for this section:
_ _ _ _ _ = Total points for this section

Divided by: _ _ _ _ _ _ (number of statements answered) = _ _ _ _ _ _
Average score for this section

Transfer your score to the ISO IEC 27001 Lead Implementer Index at the beginning of the Self-Assessment.

CRITERION #7: SUSTAIN:

INTENT: Retain the benefits.

In my belief, the answer to this question is clearly defined:

5 Strongly Agree

4 Agree

3 Neutral

2 Disagree

1 Strongly Disagree

1. What is the overall business strategy?
<--- Score

2. How do senior leaders deploy your organizations vision and values through your leadership system, to the workforce, to key suppliers and partners, and to customers and other stakeholders, as appropriate?
<--- Score

3. Is the impact that ISO IEC 27001 Lead Implementer

has shown?
<--- Score

4. Do you have a vision statement?
<--- Score

5. Is there any reason to believe the opposite of my current belief?
<--- Score

6. Design Thinking: Integrating Innovation, ISO IEC 27001 Lead Implementer Experience, and Brand Value
<--- Score

7. How can we become the company that would put us out of business?
<--- Score

8. How does ISO IEC 27001 Lead Implementer integrate with other business initiatives?
<--- Score

9. What was the last experiment we ran?
<--- Score

10. Ask yourself: how would we do this work if we only had one staff member to do it?
<--- Score

11. Who Uses What?
<--- Score

12. Who are the key stakeholders?
<--- Score

13. What is the estimated value of the project?

<--- Score

14. Think about the kind of project structure that would be appropriate for your ISO IEC 27001 Lead Implementer project. should it be formal and complex, or can it be less formal and relatively simple?
<--- Score

15. To whom do you add value?
<--- Score

16. What are strategies for increasing support and reducing opposition?
<--- Score

17. What is something you believe that nearly no one agrees with you on?
<--- Score

18. How important is ISO IEC 27001 Lead Implementer to the user organizations mission?
<--- Score

19. Is a ISO IEC 27001 Lead Implementer Team Work effort in place?
<--- Score

20. Were lessons learned captured and communicated?
<--- Score

21. What sources do you use to gather information for a ISO IEC 27001 Lead Implementer study?
<--- Score

22. If our company went out of business tomorrow, would anyone who doesn't get a paycheck here care?
<--- Score

23. How do we make it meaningful in connecting ISO IEC 27001 Lead Implementer with what users do day-to-day?
<--- Score

24. Is there any existing ISO IEC 27001 Lead Implementer governance structure?
<--- Score

25. In what ways are ISO IEC 27001 Lead Implementer vendors and us interacting to ensure safe and effective use?
<--- Score

26. Do you have an implicit bias for capital investments over people investments?
<--- Score

27. If you were responsible for initiating and implementing major changes in your organization, what steps might you take to ensure acceptance of those changes?
<--- Score

28. How do we manage ISO IEC 27001 Lead Implementer Knowledge Management (KM)?
<--- Score

29. You may have created your customer policies at a time when you lacked resources, technology wasn't up-to-snuff, or low service levels were the industry norm. Have those circumstances

changed?
<--- Score

30. How do we foster the skills, knowledge, talents, attributes, and characteristics we want to have?
<--- Score

31. Who is responsible for errors?
<--- Score

32. What role does communication play in the success or failure of a ISO IEC 27001 Lead Implementer project?
<--- Score

33. Are there any disadvantages to implementing ISO IEC 27001 Lead Implementer? There might be some that are less obvious?
<--- Score

34. What are specific ISO IEC 27001 Lead Implementer Rules to follow?
<--- Score

35. Are we changing as fast as the world around us?
<--- Score

36. Are we paying enough attention to the partners our company depends on to succeed?
<--- Score

37. If we do not follow, then how to lead?
<--- Score

38. Do you see more potential in people than they do

in themselves?
<--- Score

39. Instead of going to current contacts for new ideas, what if you reconnected with dormant contacts-- the people you used to know? If you were going reactivate a dormant tie, who would it be?
<--- Score

40. How would our PR, marketing, and social media change if we did not use outside agencies?
<--- Score

41. Is ISO IEC 27001 Lead Implementer dependent on the successful delivery of a current project?
<--- Score

42. What are we challenging, in the sense that Mac challenged the PC or Dove tackled the Beauty Myth?
<--- Score

43. Where can we break convention?
<--- Score

44. Whose voice (department, ethnic group, women, older workers, etc) might you have missed hearing from in your company, and how might you amplify this voice to create positive momentum for your business?
<--- Score

45. What are the Key enablers to make this ISO IEC 27001 Lead Implementer move?
<--- Score

46. Marketing budgets are tighter, consumers are

more skeptical, and social media has changed forever the way we talk about ISO IEC 27001 Lead Implementer. How do we gain traction?
<--- Score

47. How can you negotiate ISO IEC 27001 Lead Implementer successfully with a stubborn boss, an irate client, or a deceitful coworker?
<--- Score

48. Are we relevant? Will we be relevant five years from now? Ten?
<--- Score

49. Did my employees make progress today?
<--- Score

50. What should we stop doing?
<--- Score

51. What did we miss in the interview for the worst hire we ever made?
<--- Score

52. Who else should we help?
<--- Score

53. Who is responsible for ensuring appropriate resources (time, people and money) are allocated to ISO IEC 27001 Lead Implementer?
<--- Score

54. What are the top 3 things at the forefront of our ISO IEC 27001 Lead Implementer agendas for the next 3 years?
<--- Score

55. What business benefits will ISO IEC 27001 Lead Implementer goals deliver if achieved?
<--- Score

56. Have benefits been optimized with all key stakeholders?
<--- Score

57. Who is On the Team?
<--- Score

58. Think of your ISO IEC 27001 Lead Implementer project. what are the main functions?
<--- Score

59. What is the range of capabilities?
<--- Score

60. What is our question?
<--- Score

61. What is it like to work for me?
<--- Score

62. What trophy do we want on our mantle?
<--- Score

63. How to deal with ISO IEC 27001 Lead Implementer Changes?
<--- Score

64. Design Thinking: Integrating Innovation, ISO IEC 27001 Lead Implementer, and Brand Value
<--- Score

65. What information is critical to our organization that our executives are ignoring?

<--- Score

66. What are your most important goals for the strategic ISO IEC 27001 Lead Implementer objectives?

<--- Score

67. What is our formula for success in ISO IEC 27001 Lead Implementer ?

<--- Score

68. Is the ISO IEC 27001 Lead Implementer organization completing tasks effectively and efficiently?

<--- Score

69. How do we Lead with ISO IEC 27001 Lead Implementer in Mind?

<--- Score

70. Are new benefits received and understood?

<--- Score

71. Do we underestimate the customer's journey?

<--- Score

72. What will drive ISO IEC 27001 Lead Implementer change?

<--- Score

73. What have we done to protect our business from competitive encroachment?

<--- Score

74. How likely is it that a customer would recommend our company to a friend or colleague?
<--- Score

75. Will there be any necessary staff changes (redundancies or new hires)?
<--- Score

76. What do we do when new problems arise?
<--- Score

77. Who have we, as a company, historically been when we've been at our best?
<--- Score

78. How much does ISO IEC 27001 Lead Implementer help?
<--- Score

79. How do we provide a safe environment -physically and emotionally?
<--- Score

80. Who will provide the final approval of ISO IEC 27001 Lead Implementer deliverables?
<--- Score

81. What would I recommend my friend do if he were facing this dilemma?
<--- Score

82. How can we become more high-tech but still be high touch?
<--- Score

83. Political -is anyone trying to undermine this

project?
<--- Score

84. Who are you going to put out of business, and why?
<--- Score

85. What is the funding source for this project?
<--- Score

86. Who do we want our customers to become?
<--- Score

87. How do you determine the key elements that affect ISO IEC 27001 Lead Implementer workforce satisfaction? how are these elements determined for different workforce groups and segments?
<--- Score

88. Will it be accepted by users?
<--- Score

89. How do we maintain ISO IEC 27001 Lead Implementer's Integrity?
<--- Score

90. What are the usability implications of ISO IEC 27001 Lead Implementer actions?
<--- Score

91. Am I failing differently each time?
<--- Score

92. ISO IEC 27001 Lead Implementer Service Sales Supply Chain, Procurement, Distribution
<--- Score

93. Do we have the right capabilities and capacities?

<--- Score

94. What are all of our ISO IEC 27001 Lead Implementer domains and what do they do?

<--- Score

95. Why should people listen to you?

<--- Score

96. What am I trying to prove to myself, and how might it be hijacking my life and business success?

<--- Score

97. What is a feasible sequencing of reform initiatives over time?

<--- Score

98. How will we ensure we get what we expected?

<--- Score

99. If there were zero limitations, what would we do differently?

<--- Score

100. How long will it take to change?

<--- Score

101. How do we engage the workforce, in addition to satisfying them?

<--- Score

102. What is our competitive advantage?

<--- Score

103. What are the short and long-term ISO IEC 27001 Lead Implementer goals?

<--- Score

104. How will we insure seamless interoperability of ISO IEC 27001 Lead Implementer moving forward?

<--- Score

105. Do ISO IEC 27001 Lead Implementer rules make a reasonable demand on a users capabilities?

<--- Score

106. If you had to rebuild your organization without any traditional competitive advantages (i.e., no killer a technology, promising research, innovative product/service delivery model, etc.), how would your people have to approach their work and collaborate together in order to create the necessary conditions for success?

<--- Score

107. What is the purpose of ISO IEC 27001 Lead Implementer in relation to the mission?

<--- Score

108. Whom among your colleagues do you trust, and for what?

<--- Score

109. How is business? Why?

<--- Score

110. Has implementation been effective in reaching specified objectives?

<--- Score

111. Legal and contractual - are we allowed to do this?

<--- Score

112. What are the critical success factors?

<--- Score

113. Which individuals, teams or departments will be involved in ISO IEC 27001 Lead Implementer?

<--- Score

114. Schedule -can it be done in the given time?

<--- Score

115. Will I get fired?

<--- Score

116. Do I know what I'm doing? And who do I call if I don't?

<--- Score

117. How will we build a 100-year startup?

<--- Score

118. How to Secure ISO IEC 27001 Lead Implementer?

<--- Score

119. What happens if you do not have enough funding?

<--- Score

120. What potential megatrends could make our business model obsolete?

<--- Score

121. What is our ISO IEC 27001 Lead Implementer Strategy?

<--- Score

122. How do we keep the momentum going?

<--- Score

123. What is Effective ISO IEC 27001 Lead Implementer?

<--- Score

124. What knowledge, skills and characteristics mark a good ISO IEC 27001 Lead Implementer project manager?

<--- Score

125. How do we accomplish our long range ISO IEC 27001 Lead Implementer goals?

<--- Score

126. Who is going to care?

<--- Score

127. What are the success criteria that will indicate that ISO IEC 27001 Lead Implementer objectives have been met and the benefits delivered?

<--- Score

128. Who will determine interim and final deadlines?

<--- Score

129. Among our stronger employees, how many see themselves at the company in three years? How many would leave for a 10 percent raise from another

company?

<--- Score

130. How Do We Create Buy-in?

<--- Score

131. What one word do we want to own in the minds of our customers, employees, and partners?

<--- Score

132. What are the rules and assumptions my industry operates under? What if the opposite were true?

<--- Score

133. Are we / should we be Revolutionary or evolutionary?

<--- Score

134. Why are ISO IEC 27001 Lead Implementer skills important?

<--- Score

135. Are the assumptions believable and achievable?

<--- Score

136. In the past year, what have you done (or could you have done) to increase the accurate perception of this company/brand as ethical and honest?

<--- Score

137. What happens when a new employee joins the organization?

<--- Score

138. Why is it important to have senior

management support for a ISO IEC 27001 Lead Implementer project?

<--- Score

139. Do we have enough freaky customers in our portfolio pushing us to the limit day in and day out?

<--- Score

140. Who uses our product in ways we never expected?

<--- Score

141. If our customer were my grandmother, would I tell her to buy what we're selling?

<--- Score

142. Why don't our customers like us?

<--- Score

143. Is our strategy driving our strategy? Or is the way in which we allocate resources driving our strategy?

<--- Score

144. Who will use it?

<--- Score

145. How do I stay inspired?

<--- Score

146. What management system can we use to leverage the ISO IEC 27001 Lead Implementer experience, ideas, and concerns of the people closest to the work to be done?

<--- Score

147. How do we foster innovation?

<--- Score

148. Who will be responsible for deciding whether ISO IEC 27001 Lead Implementer goes ahead or not after the initial investigations?
<--- Score

149. What new services of functionality will be implemented next with ISO IEC 27001 Lead Implementer ?
<--- Score

150. Your reputation and success is your lifeblood, and ISO IEC 27001 Lead Implementer shows you how to stay relevant, add value, and win and retain customers
<--- Score

151. Are you satisfied with your current role? If not, what is missing from it?
<--- Score

152. What happens at this company when people fail?
<--- Score

153. When information truly is ubiquitous, when reach and connectivity are completely global, when computing resources are infinite, and when a whole new set of impossibilities are not only possible, but happening, what will that do to our business?
<--- Score

154. How Do We Know if We Are Successful?
<--- Score

155. How do we ensure that implementations of ISO IEC 27001 Lead Implementer products are

done in a way that ensures safety?

<--- Score

156. What would have to be true for the option on the table to be the best possible choice?

<--- Score

157. What are the Essentials of Internal ISO IEC 27001 Lead Implementer Management?

<--- Score

158. Is it economical; do we have the time and money?

<--- Score

159. What threat is ISO IEC 27001 Lead Implementer addressing?

<--- Score

160. How will you know that the ISO IEC 27001 Lead Implementer project has been successful?

<--- Score

161. What is an unauthorized commitment?

<--- Score

162. What is the craziest thing we can do?

<--- Score

163. Is maximizing ISO IEC 27001 Lead Implementer protection the same as minimizing ISO IEC 27001 Lead Implementer loss?

<--- Score

164. Are we making progress? and are we making progress as ISO IEC 27001 Lead Implementer

leaders?

<--- Score

165. Are the criteria for selecting recommendations stated?

<--- Score

166. Would you rather sell to knowledgeable and informed customers or to uninformed customers?

<--- Score

167. Which models, tools and techniques are necessary?

<--- Score

168. Who is the main stakeholder, with ultimate responsibility for driving ISO IEC 27001 Lead Implementer forward?

<--- Score

169. Which functions and people interact with the supplier and or customer?

<--- Score

170. What are the long-term ISO IEC 27001 Lead Implementer goals?

<--- Score

171. What are the basics of ISO IEC 27001 Lead Implementer fraud?

<--- Score

172. What does your signature ensure?

<--- Score

173. What are the gaps in my knowledge and

experience?

<--- Score

174. What may be the consequences for the performance of an organization if all stakeholders are not consulted regarding ISO IEC 27001 Lead Implementer?

<--- Score

175. If I had to leave my organization for a year and the only communication I could have with employees was a single paragraph, what would I write?

<--- Score

176. What are the challenges?

<--- Score

177. How do we go about Securing ISO IEC 27001 Lead Implementer?

<--- Score

178. Which ISO IEC 27001 Lead Implementer goals are the most important?

<--- Score

179. If we weren't already in this business, would we enter it today? And if not, what are we going to do about it?

<--- Score

180. Who sets the ISO IEC 27001 Lead Implementer standards?

<--- Score

181. What are the business goals ISO IEC 27001 Lead Implementer is aiming to achieve?

<--- Score

182. What kind of crime could a potential new hire have committed that would not only not disqualify him/her from being hired by our organization, but would actually indicate that he/she might be a particularly good fit?
<--- Score

183. What is the mission of the organization?
<--- Score

184. Who do we think the world wants us to be?
<--- Score

185. How are we doing compared to our industry?
<--- Score

186. Do we have the right people on the bus?
<--- Score

187. Where is our petri dish?
<--- Score

188. We picked a method, now what?
<--- Score

189. What is Tricky About This?
<--- Score

190. What stupid rule would we most like to kill?
<--- Score

191. How will we know if we have been successful?
<--- Score

192. What is your BATNA (best alternative to a negotiated agreement)?

<--- Score

193. Which criteria are used to determine which projects are going to be pursued or discarded?

<--- Score

194. What are internal and external ISO IEC 27001 Lead Implementer relations?

<--- Score

195. What trouble can we get into?

<--- Score

196. Do we say no to customers for no reason?

<--- Score

197. In retrospect, of the projects that we pulled the plug on, what percent do we wish had been allowed to keep going, and what percent do we wish had ended earlier?

<--- Score

198. How much contingency will be available in the budget?

<--- Score

199. If no one would ever find out about my accomplishments, how would I lead differently?

<--- Score

200. Operational - will it work?

<--- Score

201. What counts that we are not counting?

<--- Score

202. Do you keep 50% of your time unscheduled?
<--- Score

203. Do you have any supplemental information to add to this checklist?
<--- Score

204. Do we think we know, or do we know we know ?
<--- Score

205. Can we maintain our growth without detracting from the factors that have contributed to our success?
<--- Score

206. In a project to restructure ISO IEC 27001 Lead Implementer outcomes, which stakeholders would you involve?
<--- Score

207. Why should we adopt a ISO IEC 27001 Lead Implementer framework?
<--- Score

208. Is there a limit on the number of users in ISO IEC 27001 Lead Implementer ?
<--- Score

209. What will be the consequences to the stakeholder (financial, reputation etc) if ISO IEC 27001 Lead Implementer does not go ahead or fails to deliver the objectives?
<--- Score

210. Who, on the executive team or the board, has spoken to a customer recently?
<--- Score

211. If we got kicked out and the board brought in a new CEO, what would he do?
<--- Score

212. Who are four people whose careers I've enhanced?
<--- Score

213. Are there ISO IEC 27001 Lead Implementer Models?
<--- Score

214. Are assumptions made in ISO IEC 27001 Lead Implementer stated explicitly?
<--- Score

215. Who will manage the integration of tools?
<--- Score

216. How can we incorporate support to ensure safe and effective use of ISO IEC 27001 Lead Implementer into the services that we provide?
<--- Score

217. What current systems have to be understood and/or changed?
<--- Score

218. Have new benefits been realized?
<--- Score

Add up total points for this section:
_____ = Total points for this section

Divided by: _____ (number of
statements answered) = _____
Average score for this section

Transfer your score to the ISO IEC
27001 Lead Implementer Index at the
beginning of the Self-Assessment.

ISO IEC 27001 Lead Implementer and Managing Projects, Criteria for Project Managers:

1.0 Initiating Process Group: ISO IEC 27001 Lead Implementer

1. Were resources available as planned?

2. Do you understand the quality and control criteria that must be achieved for successful ISO IEC 27001 Lead Implementer project completion?

3. Are you properly tracking the progress of the ISO IEC 27001 Lead Implementer project and communicating the status to stakeholders?

4. If the risk event occurs, what will you do?

5. Are the ISO IEC 27001 Lead Implementer project team and stakeholders meeting regularly and using a meeting agenda and taking notes to accurately document what is being covered and what happened in the weekly meetings?

6. Who does what?

7. Establishment of PM Office?

8. What will be the pressing issues of tomorrow?

9. Were decisions made in a timely manner?

10. Are the changes in your ISO IEC 27001 Lead Implementer project being formally requested, analyzed, and approved by the appropriate decision makers?

11. Although the ISO IEC 27001 Lead Implementer

project manager does not directly manage procurement and contracting activities, who does manage procurement and contracting activities in your organization then if not the PM?

12. Mitigate. What will you do to minimize the impact should the risk event occur?

13. What Do You Need to Do?

14. The ISO IEC 27001 Lead Implementer project you are managing has nine stakeholders. How many channel of communications are there between these stakeholders?

15. What were the challenges that you encountered during the execution of a previous ISO IEC 27001 Lead Implementer project that you would not want to repeat?

16. Did you use a contractor or vendor?

17. The process to Manage Stakeholders is part of which process group?

18. When must it be done?

19. Who is performing the work of the ISO IEC 27001 Lead Implementer project?

20. Just how important is your work to the overall success of the ISO IEC 27001 Lead Implementer project?

1.1 Project Charter: ISO IEC 27001 Lead Implementer

21. What are some examples of a business case?

22. ISO IEC 27001 Lead Implementer project Deliverables: What is the ISO IEC 27001 Lead Implementer project going to produce?

23. Name and describe the elements that deal with providing the detail?

24. What are the assigned resources?

25. Why Executive Support?

26. What is the most common tool for helping define the detail?

27. Are there special technology requirements?

28. What date will the task finish?

29. Where and How Does the Team Fit Within the Organization Structure?

30. Run it as as a startup?

31. Customer Benefits: What customer requirements does this ISO IEC 27001 Lead Implementer project address?

32. What are the constraints?

33. Is it an improvement over existing products?

34. If finished, on what date did it finish?

35. What are the known stakeholder requirements?

36. Assumptions: What factors, for planning purposes, are you considering to be true?

37. Why use a ISO IEC 27001 Lead Implementer project charter?

38. How Do you Manage Integration?

39. What are you striving to accomplish (measurable goal(s))?

40. What's in it for you?

1.2 Stakeholder Register: ISO IEC 27001 Lead Implementer

41. Who is Managing Stakeholder Engagement?

42. Who are the stakeholders?

43. Is Your Organization Ready for Change?

44. How should employers make their voices heard?

45. How will Reports Be Created?

46. How Big is the Gap?

47. What is the power of the stakeholder?

48. How much influence do they have on the ISO IEC 27001 Lead Implementer project?

49. What & Why?

50. What are the major ISO IEC 27001 Lead Implementer project milestones requiring communications or providing communications opportunities?

51. Who wants to talk about Security?

52. What opportunities exist to provide communications?

1.3 Stakeholder Analysis Matrix: ISO IEC 27001 Lead Implementer

53. Are there people whose voices or interests in the issue may not be heard?

54. Effects on core activities, distraction?

55. What are innovative aspects of the organization?

56. Continuity, supply chain robustness?

57. What actions can be taken to reduce or mitigate risk?

58. Who will be responsible for managing the outcome?

59. What is our Advocacy Strategy?

60. Accreditations, etc?

61. Economy - home, abroad?

62. Vulnerable Groups; Who are the vulnerable groups that might be affected by the ISO IEC 27001 Lead Implementer project?

63. Advantages of proposition?

64. Who are potential allies and opponents?

65. Who has been involved in the area (thematic or

geographic) in the past?

66. Usps (unique selling points)?

67. IT developments?

68. Sustaining internal capabilities?

69. How do customers express needs?

70. Do the stakeholders goals and expectations support or conflict with the ISO IEC 27001 Lead Implementer project goals?

71. Which conditions out of the control of the management are crucial to contribute for the achievement of the development objective?

2.0 Planning Process Group: ISO IEC 27001 Lead Implementer

72. Is the ISO IEC 27001 Lead Implementer project supported by national and/or local organizations?

73. To what extent do the intervention objectives and strategies of the ISO IEC 27001 Lead Implementer project respond to the organizations plans?

74. Will the products created live up to the necessary quality?

75. How should their needs be met?

76. If you are late, will anybody notice?

77. What is the difference between the early schedule and late schedule?

78. Professionals want to know what is expected from them; what are the deliverables?

79. How Will You Know You Did It?

80. If a risk event occurs, what will you do?

81. How do you integrate ISO IEC 27001 Lead Implementer project Planning with the Iterative/Evolutionary SDLC?

82. To what extent have public/private national resources and/or counterparts been mobilized to

contribute to the programmes objective and produce results and impacts?

83. Just how important is your work to the overall success of the ISO IEC 27001 Lead Implementer project?

84. Is the duration of the programme sufficient to ensure a cycle that will ISO IEC 27001 Lead Implementer project the sustainability of the interventions?

85. Did you read it correctly?

86. How well do the team follow the chosen processes?

87. Did the programme design/ implementation strategy adequately address the planning stage necessary to set up structures, hire staff etc.?

88. How Will You Do It?

89. What Will You Do?

90. What makes your ISO IEC 27001 Lead Implementer project successful?

91. Explanation: Is what the ISO IEC 27001 Lead Implementer project intents to solve a hard question?

2.1 Project Management Plan: ISO IEC 27001 Lead Implementer

92. Why Change?

93. Do there need to be organizational changes?

94. Are calculations and results of analyses essentially correct?

95. Who is the ISO IEC 27001 Lead Implementer project Manager?

96. Do the proposed changes from the ISO IEC 27001 Lead Implementer project include any significant risks to safety?

97. Has the selected plan been formulated using cost effectiveness and incremental analysis techniques?

98. When is the ISO IEC 27001 Lead Implementer project management plan created?

99. How do you organize the costs in the ISO IEC 27001 Lead Implementer project management plan?

100. What data/reports/tools/etc. do program managers need?

101. Where does all this information come from?

102. What are the assumptions?

103. Are there any windfall benefits that would accrue to the ISO IEC 27001 Lead Implementer project sponsor or other parties?

104. Are there non-structural buyout or relocation recommendations?

105. What is ISO IEC 27001 Lead Implementer project Scope Management?

106. What is the business need?

107. Does the selected plan protect privacy?

108. Who Manages Integration?

109. What are the training needs?

2.2 Scope Management Plan: ISO IEC 27001 Lead Implementer

110. For which criterion is it tolerable not to meet the original parameters?

111. Has a proper ISO IEC 27001 Lead Implementer project work location been established that will allow the team to work together with user personnel?

112. Are alternatives safe, functional, constructible, economical, reasonable and sustainable?

113. Have the procedures for identifying variances from estimates & adjusting the detailed work program been followed?

114. Is mitigation authorized or recommended?

115. Are the payment terms being followed?

116. Alignment to strategic goals & objectives?

117. Are updated ISO IEC 27001 Lead Implementer project time & resource estimates reasonable based on the current ISO IEC 27001 Lead Implementer project stage?

118. The greatest degree of uncertainty is encountered during which phase of the ISO IEC 27001 Lead Implementer project life cycle?

119. Are risk triggers captured?

120. What is the need the ISO IEC 27001 Lead Implementer project will address?

121. Are the schedule estimates reasonable given the ISO IEC 27001 Lead Implementer project?

122. How many changes are you making?

123. How do you plan to control Scope Creep?

124. Have ISO IEC 27001 Lead Implementer project management standards and procedures been identified / established and documented?

125. Is there a Steering Committee in place?

126. Are staff skills known and available for each task?

127. Is there a scope management plan that includes how ISO IEC 27001 Lead Implementer project scope will be defined, developed, monitored, validated and controlled?

2.3 Requirements Management Plan: ISO IEC 27001 Lead Implementer

128. Is there formal agreement on who has authority to approve a change in requirements?

129. Who will finally present the work or product(s) for acceptance?

130. How will the information be distributed?

131. Controlling ISO IEC 27001 Lead Implementer project requirements involves monitoring the status of the ISO IEC 27001 Lead Implementer project requirements and managing changes to the requirements. Who is responsible for monitoring and tracking the ISO IEC 27001 Lead Implementer project requirements?

132. Do you know which stakeholders will participate in the requirements effort?

133. The WBS is developed as part of a Joint Planning session. But how do you know that youve done this right?

134. Will you document changes to requirements?

135. Do you expect stakeholders to be cooperative?

136. Do you understand the role that each stakeholder will play in the requirements process?

137. Describe the process for rejecting the ISO IEC 27001 Lead Implementer project requirements. Who has the authority to reject ISO IEC 27001 Lead Implementer project requirements?

138. Are all the stakeholders ready for the transition into the user community?

139. How detailed should the ISO IEC 27001 Lead Implementer project get?

140. How will you communicate scheduled tasks to other team members?

141. Who is responsible for quantifying the ISO IEC 27001 Lead Implementer project requirements?

142. Has the requirements team been instructed in the Change Control process?

143. Did you use declarative statements?

144. After the requirements are gathered and set forth on the requirements register, they're little more than a laundry list of items. Some may be duplicates, some might conflict with others and some will be too broad or too vague to understand. Describe how the requirements will be analyzed. Who will perform the analysis?

145. What Went Wrong?

146. Which hardware or software, related to, or as outcome of the ISO IEC 27001 Lead Implementer project is new to the organization?

147. Could inaccurate or incomplete requirements in this ISO IEC 27001 Lead Implementer project create a serious risk for the business?

2.4 Requirements Documentation: ISO IEC 27001 Lead Implementer

148. What is the risk associated with the technology?

149. What is a show stopper in the requirements?

150. Does the system provide the functions which best support the customers needs?

151. Are there legal issues?

152. Is the origin of the requirement clearly stated?

153. Basic work/Business process; high-level, what is being touched?

154. How do you know when a Requirement is accurate enough?

155. How will the proposed ISO IEC 27001 Lead Implementer project help?

156. What are the potential disadvantages/ advantages?

157. What are the acceptance criteria?

158. Does your company restrict technical alternatives?

159. What is Effective documentation?

160. How much testing do you need to do to prove that my system is safe?

161. Is the requirement realistically testable?

162. Is the requirement properly understood?

163. How can you document system requirements?

164. How linear / iterative is your Requirements Gathering process (or will it be)?

165. What kind of entity is a problem ?

166. Consistency. Are there any requirements conflicts?

167. Are all functions required by the customer included?

2.5 Requirements Traceability Matrix: ISO IEC 27001 Lead Implementer

168. Why use a WBS?

169. How Do you Manage Scope?

170. What are the chronologies, contingencies, consequences, criteria?

171. What percentage of ISO IEC 27001 Lead Implementer projects are producing traceability matrices between requirements and other work products?

172. What is the WBS?

173. Is there a requirements traceability process in place?

174. How will it affect the stakeholders personally in their career?

175. Why Do you Manage Scope?

176. Will you use a Requirements Traceability Matrix?

177. How small is small enough?

178. Do we have a clear understanding of all subcontracts in place?

179. Describe the process for approving requirements

so they can be added to the traceability matrix and ISO IEC 27001 Lead Implementer project work can be performed. Will the ISO IEC 27001 Lead Implementer project requirements become approved in writing?

2.6 Project Scope Statement: ISO IEC 27001 Lead Implementer

180. What is the product of this ISO IEC 27001 Lead Implementer project?

181. Has a method and process for requirement tracking been developed?

182. Is the organization structure appropriate for the ISO IEC 27001 Lead Implementer projects size and complexity?

183. Is an Issue Management Process documented and filed?

184. How often will scope changes be reviewed?

185. Once its defined, what is the stability of the ISO IEC 27001 Lead Implementer project scope?

186. Is the plan for the organization of the ISO IEC 27001 Lead Implementer project resources adequate?

187. Have the Configuration Management functions been assigned?

188. How will you verify the accuracy of the work of the ISO IEC 27001 Lead Implementer project, and what constitutes acceptance of the deliverables?

189. Write a brief purpose statement for this ISO IEC 27001 Lead Implementer project. Include a business

justification statement. What is the product of this ISO IEC 27001 Lead Implementer project?

190. Will all ISO IEC 27001 Lead Implementer project issues be unconditionally tracked through the issue resolution process?

191. Is the plan for ISO IEC 27001 Lead Implementer project resources adequate?

192. Is the scope of your ISO IEC 27001 Lead Implementer project well defined?

193. Is there a Quality Assurance Plan documented and filed?

194. Identify how your team and you will create the ISO IEC 27001 Lead Implementer project scope statement and the work breakdown structure (WBS). Document how you will create the ISO IEC 27001 Lead Implementer project scope statement and WBS, and make sure you answer the following questions: In defining ISO IEC 27001 Lead Implementer project scope and the WBS, will you and your ISO IEC 27001 Lead Implementer project team be using methods defined by your organization, methods defined by the ISO IEC 27001 Lead Implementer project management office (PMO), or other methods?

195. Will all tasks resulting from issues be entered into the ISO IEC 27001 Lead Implementer project Plan and tracked through the plan?

196. Is there a Change Management Board?

197. Will an issue form be in use?

198. Is there a baseline plan against which to measure progress?

199. Were potential customers involved early in the planning process?

2.7 Assumption and Constraint Log: ISO IEC 27001 Lead Implementer

200. Are best practices and metrics employed to identify issues, progress, performance, etc.?

201. No superfluous information or marketing narrative?

202. Are there procedures in place to effectively manage interdependencies with other ISO IEC 27001 Lead Implementer projects / systems?

203. What if failure during recovery?

204. Is there adequate stakeholder participation for the vetting of requirements definition, changes and management?

205. Can you perform this task or activity in a more effective manner?

206. What other teams / processes would be impacted by changes to the current process, and how?

207. What would you gain if you spent time working to improve this process?

208. Is the Steering Committee active in ISO IEC 27001 Lead Implementer project oversight?

209. What Threats might prevent us from getting there?

210. Contradictory information between document sections?

211. Are there unnecessary steps that are creating bottlenecks and/or causing people to wait?

212. Should factors be unpredictable over time?

213. Does a specific action and/or state that is known to violate security policy occur?

214. How do you design an auditing system?

215. What to do at recovery?

216. Were the system requirements formally reviewed prior to initiating the design phase?

217. Have you eliminated all duplicative tasks or manual efforts, where appropriate?

218. Are funding and staffing resource estimates sufficiently detailed and documented for use in planning and tracking the ISO IEC 27001 Lead Implementer project?

219. What do you log?

2.8 Work Breakdown Structure: ISO IEC 27001 Lead Implementer

220. Why would you develop a Work Breakdown Structure?

221. What is the probability that the ISO IEC 27001 Lead Implementer project duration will exceed xx weeks?

222. Where does it take place?

223. How Far Down?

224. When does it have to be done?

225. Is it still viable?

226. How much detail?

227. What is the probability of completing the ISO IEC 27001 Lead Implementer project in less that xx days?

228. How will you and your ISO IEC 27001 Lead Implementer project team define the ISO IEC 27001 Lead Implementer projects scope and work breakdown structure?

229. Do you need another level?

230. When would you develop a Work Breakdown Structure?

231. How many levels?

232. Can you make it?

233. Is it a change in scope?

234. How big is a work-package?

235. When do you stop?

236. Is the Work breakdown Structure (WBS) defined and is the scope of the ISO IEC 27001 Lead Implementer project clear with assigned deliverable owners?

237. What has to be done?

238. Why is it useful?

239. Who has to do it?

2.9 WBS Dictionary: ISO IEC 27001 Lead Implementer

240. What is the goal?

241. Intermediate schedules, as required, which provide a logical sequence from the master schedule to the control account level?

242. Are all elements of indirect expense identified to overhead cost budgets of ISO IEC 27001 Lead Implementer projections?

243. Are estimates of costs at completion utilized in determining contract funding requirements and reporting them?

244. Are overhead cost budgets established for each organization which has authority to incur overhead costs?

245. Do the lines of authority for incurring indirect costs correspond to the lines of responsibility for management control of the same components of costs?

246. Is cost performance measurement at the point in time most suitable for the category of material involved, but no earlier than the time of actual receipt of material?

247. Detailed schedules which support control account and work package start and completion

dates/events?

248. Are time-phased budgets established for planning and control of level of effort activity by category of resource; for example, type of manpower and/or material?

249. Changes in the overhead pool and/or organization structures?

250. Budgeted cost for work performed?

251. Are data elements summarized through the functional organizational structure for progressively higher levels of management?

252. Changes in the current direct and ISO IEC 27001 Lead Implementer projected base?

253. Actual cost of work performed?

254. Do work packages reflect the actual way in which the work will be done and are they meaningful products or management-oriented subdivisions of a higher level element of work?

255. Are work packages reasonably short in time duration or do they have adequate objective indicators/milestones to minimize subjectivity of the in process work evaluation?

256. Changes in the nature of the overhead requirements?

257. Are material costs reported within the same period as that in which BCWP is earned for that

material?

258. Major functional areas of contract effort?

259. Contemplated overhead expenditure for each period based on the best information currently available?

2.10 Schedule Management Plan: ISO IEC 27001 Lead Implementer

260. Is the plan consistent with industry best practices?

261. Has the schedule been baselined?

262. Have the key elements of a coherent ISO IEC 27001 Lead Implementer project management strategy been established?

263. Are updated ISO IEC 27001 Lead Implementer project time & resource estimates reasonable based on the current ISO IEC 27001 Lead Implementer project stage?

264. Is the firm certified as a broker of the products/supplies?

265. Has process improvement efforts been completed before requirements efforts begin?

266. Are actuals compared against estimates to analyze and correct variances?

267. Has a Quality Assurance Plan been developed for the ISO IEC 27001 Lead Implementer project?

268. Are adequate resources provided for the quality assurance function?

269. Is the development plan and/or process

documented?

270. Do ISO IEC 27001 Lead Implementer project teams & team members report on status / activities / progress?

271. Cost / Benefit Analysis?

272. Has the IMS content been baselined and is it adequately controlled?

273. Goal: Is the schedule feasible and at what cost?

274. Are ISO IEC 27001 Lead Implementer project team members involved in detailed estimating and scheduling?

275. Does the ISO IEC 27001 Lead Implementer project have quality set of schedule BOEs?

276. Is there a procedure for management, control and release of schedule margin?

277. Identify the amount of schedule variation that triggers a warning. What happens if a warning is triggered?

278. Is ISO IEC 27001 Lead Implementer project status reviewed with the steering and executive teams at appropriate intervals?

279. What tools and techniques will be used to estimate activity resources?

2.11 Activity List: ISO IEC 27001 Lead Implementer

280. What are the critical bottleneck activities?

281. How difficult will it be to do specific activities on this ISO IEC 27001 Lead Implementer project?

282. How detailed should a ISO IEC 27001 Lead Implementer project get?

283. In what sequence?

284. Is infrastructure setup part of your ISO IEC 27001 Lead Implementer project?

285. When will the work be performed?

286. What went well?

287. Where will it be performed?

288. What are you counting on?

289. Is there anything planned that doesn t need to be here?

290. Are the required resources available or need to be acquired?

291. Can you determine the activity that must finish, before this activity can start?

292. What did not go as well?

293. How much slack is available in the ISO IEC 27001 Lead Implementer project?

294. What will be performed?

295. What is the LF and LS for each activity?

296. How will it be performed?

297. What is the total time required to complete the ISO IEC 27001 Lead Implementer project if no delays occur?

298. What is the least expensive way to complete the ISO IEC 27001 Lead Implementer project within 40 weeks?

2.12 Activity Attributes: ISO IEC 27001 Lead Implementer

299. Have constraints been applied to the start and finish milestones for the phases?

300. What activity do you think you should spend the most time on?

301. Whats the general pattern here?

302. Have you identified the Activity Leveling Priority code value on each activity?

303. How difficult will it be to complete specific activities on this ISO IEC 27001 Lead Implementer project?

304. Time for overtime?

305. How Do you Manage Time?

306. Has management defined a definite timeframe for the turnaround or ISO IEC 27001 Lead Implementer project window?

307. How Much Activity Detail Is Required?

308. Can more resources be added?

309. What is the organization s history in doing similar activities?

310. How many days do you need to complete the work scope with a limit of X number of resources?

311. Which method produces the more accurate cost assignment?

312. How many resources do you need to complete the work scope within a limit of X number of days?

313. Activity: Whats Missing?

314. Do you feel very comfortable with your prediction?

315. What conclusions/generalizations can you draw from this?

316. Where else does it apply?

2.13 Milestone List: ISO IEC 27001 Lead Implementer

317. How soon can the activity start?

318. Describe the concept of the technology, product or service that will be or has been developed. How will it be used?

319. How late can each activity be finished and started?

320. Own known vulnerabilities?

321. Timescales, deadlines and pressures?

322. New USPs?

323. Describe the industry you are in and the market growth opportunities. What is the market for your technology, product or service?

324. What specific improvements did you make to the ISO IEC 27001 Lead Implementer project proposal since the previous time?

325. Do you foresee any technical risks or developmental challenges?

326. Can you derive how soon can the whole ISO IEC 27001 Lead Implementer project finish?

327. What is the market for your technology, product

or service?

328. Identify critical paths (one or more) and which activities are on the critical path?

329. Milestone pages should display the UserID of the person who added the milestone. Does a report or query exist that provides this audit information?

330. Level of the Innovation?

331. Competitive advantages?

332. Legislative effects?

2.14 Network Diagram: ISO IEC 27001 Lead Implementer

333. What are the tools?

334. If X is long, what would be the completion time if you break X into two parallel parts of y weeks and z weeks?

335. What job or jobs precede it?

336. Which type of network diagram allows you to depict four types of dependencies?

337. Where Do Schedules Come From?

338. How confident can you be in our milestone dates and the delivery date?

339. Planning: who, how long, what to do?

340. What is the probability of completing the ISO IEC 27001 Lead Implementer project in less that xx days?

341. Are the Gantt Chart and/or Network Diagram updated periodically and used to assess the overall ISO IEC 27001 Lead Implementer project timetable?

342. What are the Major Administrative Issues?

343. If the ISO IEC 27001 Lead Implementer project network diagram cannot change but you have extra personnel resources, what is the BEST thing to do?

344. If a current contract exists, can you provide the vendor name, contract start, and contract expiration date?

345. Will crashing x weeks return more in benefits than it costs?

346. What is the completion time?

347. What is the lowest cost to complete this ISO IEC 27001 Lead Implementer project in xx weeks?

348. What controls the start and finish of a job?

349. Why must you schedule milestones, such as reviews, throughout the ISO IEC 27001 Lead Implementer project?

350. What activities must follow this activity?

351. What are the Key Success Factors?

2.15 Activity Resource Requirements: ISO IEC 27001 Lead Implementer

352. Anything else?

353. How many signatures do you require on a check and does this match what is in your policy and procedures?

354. How do you handle petty cash?

355. Other support in specific areas?

356. Why do you do that?

357. When does Monitoring Begin?

358. Organizational Applicability?

359. Are there unresolved issues that need to be addressed?

360. Do you use tools like decomposition and rolling-wave planning to produce the activity list and other outputs?

361. Which logical relationship does the PDM use most often?

362. What are constraints that you might find during the Human Resource Planning process?

363. What is the Work Plan Standard?

2.16 Resource Breakdown Structure: ISO IEC 27001 Lead Implementer

364. What Is ISO IEC 27001 Lead Implementer project Communication Management?

365. Why Time Management?

366. What s the difference between % Complete and % work?

367. What is the number one predictor of a groups productivity?

368. When do they need the information?

369. Who is allowed to perform which functions?

370. Changes Based on Input from Stakeholders?

371. What is the organizations history in doing similar activities?

372. Who will use the system?

373. Who is allowed to see what data about which resources?

374. How can this help you with team building?

375. Why Do you Do It?

376. How difficult will it be to do specific activities on

this ISO IEC 27001 Lead Implementer project?

377. Who needs what information?

378. What are the requirements for resource data?

379. Any Changes from Stakeholders?

380. What Went Right?

2.17 Activity Duration Estimates: ISO IEC 27001 Lead Implementer

381. Do they make sense?

382. What questions do you have about the sample documents provided?

383. Is a contract change control system defined to manage changes to contract terms and conditions?

384. How do functionality, system outputs, performance, reliability, and maintainability requirements affect quality planning?

385. Which would be the NEXT thing for the ISO IEC 27001 Lead Implementer project manager to do?

386. Describe a ISO IEC 27001 Lead Implementer project that suffered from scope creep. Could it have been avoided?

387. Can they use those?

388. What is the BEST thing for the ISO IEC 27001 Lead Implementer project manager to do?

389. What are some of the largest companies that provide information technology outsourcing services?

390. Does a process exist to determine which risk events to accept and which events to disregard?

391. What functions does this software provide that cannot be done easily using other tools such as a spreadsheet or database?

392. If you plan to take the PMP exam soon, what should you do to prepare?

393. If the optimistic estimate for an activity is 12days, and the pessimistic estimate is 18days, what is the standard deviation of this activity?

394. Do an Internet search on earning PMP certification. Be sure to search for Yahoo Groups related to this topic. What are some of the options you found to help people prepare for the exam?

395. What are some crucial elements of a good ISO IEC 27001 Lead Implementer project plan?

396. How does poking fun at technical professionals communications skills impact the industry and educational programs?

397. Are adjustments implemented to correct or prevent defects?

398. What is the critical path for this ISO IEC 27001 Lead Implementer project and how long is it?

399. What are some of the typical challenges ISO IEC 27001 Lead Implementer project teams face during each of the five process groups?

400. What are the nine areas of expertise?

2.18 Duration Estimating Worksheet: ISO IEC 27001 Lead Implementer

401. What is the total time required to complete the ISO IEC 27001 Lead Implementer project if no delays occur?

402. Done before proceeding with this activity or what can be done concurrently?

403. Will the ISO IEC 27001 Lead Implementer project collaborate with the local community and leverage resources?

404. Why estimate time and cost?

405. When do the individual activities need to start and finish?

406. Is this operation cost effective?

407. Is the ISO IEC 27001 Lead Implementer project responsive to community need?

408. Does the ISO IEC 27001 Lead Implementer project provide innovative ways for Veterans to overcome obstacles or deliver better outcomes?

409. When, then?

410. Do any colleagues have experience with the company and/or RFPs?

411. Science = Process: Remember the Scientific Method?

412. What info is needed?

413. What questions do you have?

414. How can the ISO IEC 27001 Lead Implementer project be displayed graphically to better visualize the activities?

415. Why Estimate Costs?

416. Define the work as completely as possible. What work will be included in the ISO IEC 27001 Lead Implementer project?

417. For other activities, how much delay can be tolerated?

418. What is the probability the ISO IEC 27001 Lead Implementer project can be completed in 47 weeks?

2.19 Project Schedule: ISO IEC 27001 Lead Implementer

419. Why or why not?

420. How can you address that situation?

421. How can you minimize or control changes to ISO IEC 27001 Lead Implementer project schedules?

422. A master ISO IEC 27001 Lead Implementer project schedule?

423. Are all remaining durations correct?

424. Is the ISO IEC 27001 Lead Implementer project schedule available for all ISO IEC 27001 Lead Implementer project team members to review?

425. Verify that the update is accurate. Are all remaining durations correct?

426. Is infrastructure setup part of your ISO IEC 27001 Lead Implementer project?

427. Are there activities that came from a template or previous ISO IEC 27001 Lead Implementer project that are not applicable on this phase of this ISO IEC 27001 Lead Implementer project?

428. Have all ISO IEC 27001 Lead Implementer project delays been adequately accounted for, communicated to all stakeholders and adjustments made in overall

ISO IEC 27001 Lead Implementer project schedule?

429. Why is this particularly bad?

430. Are the original ISO IEC 27001 Lead Implementer project schedule and budget realistic?

431. How detailed should a ISO IEC 27001 Lead Implementer project get?

432. How do you manage ISO IEC 27001 Lead Implementer project Risk?

433. Should you have a test for each code module?

434. Was the ISO IEC 27001 Lead Implementer project schedule reviewed by all stakeholders and formally accepted?

435. Is there a Schedule Management Plan that establishes the criteria and activities for developing, monitoring and controlling the ISO IEC 27001 Lead Implementer project schedule?

436. Understand the constraints used in preparing the schedule. Are activities connected because logic dictates the order in which others occur?

437. What is the most mis-scheduled part of process?

2.20 Cost Management Plan: ISO IEC 27001 Lead Implementer

438. Is there any form of automated support for Issues Management?

439. Mitigation – Based on the action, cost and probability of success, will the mitigation be made?

440. Has a Resource Management Plan been created?

441. Has a sponsor been identified?

442. Ranged estimates?

443. Are meeting minutes captured and sent out after the meeting?

444. Are multiple estimation methods being employed?

445. Why Do you Manage Cost?

446. Have key stakeholders been identified?

447. Environmental management – What changes in statutory environmental compliance requirements are anticipated during the ISO IEC 27001 Lead Implementer project?

448. Is ISO IEC 27001 Lead Implementer project status reviewed with the steering and executive teams at appropriate intervals?

449. Is there an onboarding process in place?

450. Does the Resource Management Plan include a personnel development plan?

451. Has a capability assessment been conducted?

452. Escalation Criteria Met?

453. Does a documented ISO IEC 27001 Lead Implementer project organizational policy & plan (i.e. governance model) exist?

454. Is a PMO (ISO IEC 27001 Lead Implementer project Management Office) in place and provide oversight to the ISO IEC 27001 Lead Implementer project?

455. Are ISO IEC 27001 Lead Implementer project contact logs kept up to date?

456. Have all team members been part of identifying risks?

2.21 Activity Cost Estimates: ISO IEC 27001 Lead Implementer

457. One way to define activities is to consider how organization employees describe jobs to families and friends. You basically want to know, What do you do?

458. Vac -variance at completion, how much over/under budget do you expect to be?

459. How do you treat administrative costs in the activity inventory?

460. What is the last item a ISO IEC 27001 Lead Implementer project manager must do to finalize ISO IEC 27001 Lead Implementer project close-out?

461. Performance bond should always provide what part of the contract value?

462. Does the estimator estimate by task or by person?

463. Scope statement only direct or indirect costs as well?

464. Which contract type places the most risk on the seller?

465. How Do you Manage Cost?

466. What Defines a Successful ISO IEC 27001 Lead Implementer project?

467. What is Procurement?

468. What makes a good expected result statement?

469. How and when do you enter into ISO IEC 27001 Lead Implementer project Procurement Management?

470. Estimated cost?

471. What is the organization s history in doing similar tasks?

472. Is costing method consistent with study goals?

473. Was it performed on time?

474. Based on your ISO IEC 27001 Lead Implementer project communication management plan, what worked well?

475. Are data needed on characteristics of care?

2.22 Cost Estimating Worksheet: ISO IEC 27001 Lead Implementer

476. What will others want?

477. Does the ISO IEC 27001 Lead Implementer project provide innovative ways for stakeholders to overcome obstacles or deliver better outcomes?

478. Who is best positioned to know and assist in identifying such factors?

479. What additional ISO IEC 27001 Lead Implementer project(s) could be initiated as a result of this ISO IEC 27001 Lead Implementer project?

480. What is the estimated labor cost today based upon this information?

481. Will the ISO IEC 27001 Lead Implementer project collaborate with the local community and leverage resources?

482. Identify the timeframe necessary to monitor progress and collect data to determine how the selected measure has changed?

483. Can a trend be established from historical performance data on the selected measure and are the criteria for using trend analysis or forecasting methods met?

484. What happens to any remaining funds not used?

485. Value Pocket Identification & Quantification What Are Value Pockets?

486. Is the ISO IEC 27001 Lead Implementer project responsive to community need?

487. What Can Be Included?

488. How will the results be shared and to whom?

489. Is it feasible to establish a control group arrangement?

490. What costs are to be estimated?

491. Ask: are others positioned to know, are others credible, and will others cooperate?

492. What is the purpose of estimating?

2.23 Cost Baseline: ISO IEC 27001 Lead Implementer

493. Are procedures defined by which the cost baseline may be changed?

494. Have all approved changes to the ISO IEC 27001 Lead Implementer project requirement been identified and impact on the performance, cost, and schedule baselines documented?

495. Does the suggested change request represent a desired enhancement to the products functionality?

496. Where Do Changes Come From?

497. Are there contingencies or conditions related to the acceptance?

498. Have you identified skills that are missing from your team?

499. Does it impact schedule, cost, quality?

500. Has the ISO IEC 27001 Lead Implementer project (or ISO IEC 27001 Lead Implementer project phase) been evaluated against each objective established in the product description and Integrated ISO IEC 27001 Lead Implementer project Plan?

501. Who will use such metrics ?

502. At which frequency ?

503. ISO IEC 27001 Lead Implementer project Goals -should others be reconsidered?

504. What s the reality?

505. Has operations management formally accepted responsibility for operating and maintaining the product(s) or service(s) delivered by the ISO IEC 27001 Lead Implementer project?

506. What is the consequence?

507. What is the most important thing to do next to make your ISO IEC 27001 Lead Implementer project successful?

508. Verify business objectives. Are others appropriate, and well-articulated?

509. Have all approved changes to the cost baseline been identified and impact on the ISO IEC 27001 Lead Implementer project documented?

510. What would some of the life cycle costs be?

511. What Strengths do you have?

2.24 Quality Management Plan: ISO IEC 27001 Lead Implementer

512. How long do you retain data?

513. What type of in-house testing do you conduct?

514. Is this a Requirement?

515. How does your organization decide what to measure?

516. Is it necessary?

517. How are changes to procedures made?

518. How do senior leaders create an environment that encourages learning and innovation?

519. How does your organization use comparative data and information to improve organizational performance?

520. Is there a Quality Management Plan?

521. How are calibration records kept?

522. How is the information recorded?

523. Are you following the quality standards?

524. Do you keep back-up copies of any data?

525. What are your organizations current levels and trends for those measures related to employee wellbeing, satisfaction, and development?

526. Show/provide copy of procedures for taking field notes?

527. Are QMPs Good Forever?

528. How does your organization design processes to ensure others meet customer and others requirements?

529. Who do you send data to?

530. What are your organizations current levels and trends for those measures related to customer satisfaction/ dissatisfaction and product/service performance?

2.25 Quality Metrics: ISO IEC 27001 Lead Implementer

531. Is a risk containment plan in place?

532. Do you know how much profit a 10% decrease in waste would generate?

533. When is the security analysis testing complete?

534. What metrics are important and most beneficial to measure?

535. Are quality metrics defined?

536. What forces exist that would cause them to change?

537. Product Availability ?

538. How do you calculate such metrics?

539. What does this tell us?

540. What makes a visualization memorable?

541. Did the team meet the ISO IEC 27001 Lead Implementer project success criteria documented in the Quality Metrics Matrix?

542. How effective are your security tests?

543. Has it met internal or external standards?

544. Which report did you use to create the data you are submitting?

545. Has trace of defects been initiated?

546. How does one achieve stability?

547. The metrics–whats being considered?

548. Did evaluation start on time?

549. If the defect rate during testing is substantially higher than that of the previous release (or a similar product), then ask: Did you plan for and actually improve testing effectiveness?

550. Where did complaints, returns and warranty claims come from?

2.26 Process Improvement Plan: ISO IEC 27001 Lead Implementer

551. Are you meeting the quality standards?

552. What is the return on investment?

553. Where do you want to be?

554. Does explicit definition of the measures exist?

555. Does our process ensure quality?

556. If a Process Improvement Framework Is Being Used, Which Elements Will Help the Problems and Goals Listed?

557. The motive is determined by asking, Why do I want to achieve this goal?

558. How Do you Manage Quality?

559. Modeling current processes is great, but will you ever see a return on that investment?

560. Why Quality Management?

561. What makes people good SPI coaches?

562. What Actions Are Needed to Address the Problems and Achieve the Goals?

563. How do you measure?

564. What Is the Test-Cycle Concept?

565. Has a process guide to collect the data been developed?

566. What personnel are the change agents for your initiative?

567. What Lessons Have you Learned So Far?

568. To elicit goal statements, do you ask a question such as, What do you want to achieve?

569. Why do you want to achieve the goal?

2.27 Responsibility Assignment Matrix: ISO IEC 27001 Lead Implementer

570. Budgets assigned to control accounts?

571. Does the scheduling system identify in a timely manner the status of work?

572. How Do you Manage Human Resources?

573. Is accountability placed at the lowest-possible level within the ISO IEC 27001 Lead Implementer project so that decisions can be made at that level?

574. How many people do you need?

575. Are People Afraid to Let You Know When others Are Under Allocated?

576. Budgets assigned to major functional organizations?

577. What does WBS accomplish?

578. What materials and procurements needed?

579. What expertise is not available in your department?

580. With too many people labeled as doing the work, are there too many hands involved?

581. Is work progressively subdivided into detailed work packages as requirements are defined?

582. How many hours by each staff member/rate?

583. Ideas for Developing Soft Skills at your organization?

584. Does the contractors system include procedures for measuring the performance of critical subcontractors?

585. How do you manage remotely to staff in other Divisions?

586. Wbs elements contractually specified for reporting of status (lowest level only)?

2.28 Roles and Responsibilities: ISO IEC 27001 Lead Implementer

587. What is working well within your organizations performance management system?

588. Does the team have access to and ability to use data analysis tools?

589. What expectations were met?

590. Is feedback clearly communicated and non-judgmental?

591. What should you do now to prepare yourself for a promotion, increased responsibilities or a different job?

592. Are our budgets supportive of a culture of quality data?

593. Implementation of actions: Who are the responsible units?

594. How is your work-life balance?

595. Concern: where are you limited or have no authority, where you cant influence?

596. Accountabilities: What are the roles and responsibilities of individual team members?

597. Have you ever been a part of this team?

598. Who is responsible for each task?

599. Does our vision/mission support a culture of quality data?

600. Once the responsibilities are defined for the ISO IEC 27001 Lead Implementer project, have the deliverables, roles and responsibilities been clearly communicated to every participant?

601. Whats working well?

602. Who is responsible for implementation activities and where will the functions, roles and responsibilities be defined?

603. Are our policies supportive of a culture of quality data?

604. Influence: What areas of organizational decision making are you able to influence when you do not have authority to make the final decision?

605. Attainable / Achievable: The goal is attainable; can you actually accomplish the goal?

606. What should you do now to prepare for your career 5+ years from now?

2.29 Human Resource Management Plan: ISO IEC 27001 Lead Implementer

607. Have ISO IEC 27001 Lead Implementer project management standards and procedures been identified / established and documented?

608. Are issues raised, assessed, actioned, and resolved in a timely and efficient manner?

609. What were things that you did very well and want to do the same again on the next ISO IEC 27001 Lead Implementer project?

610. Is there a set of procedures to capture, analyze and act on quality metrics?

611. Is a Stakeholder Management plan in place that covers topics?

612. Is the assigned ISO IEC 27001 Lead Implementer project manager a PMP (Certified ISO IEC 27001 Lead Implementer project manager) and experienced?

613. Have stakeholder accountabilities & responsibilities been clearly defined?

614. Is the structure for tracking the ISO IEC 27001 Lead Implementer project schedule well defined and assigned to a specific individual?

615. Do ISO IEC 27001 Lead Implementer project managers participating in the ISO IEC 27001 Lead

Implementer project know the ISO IEC 27001 Lead Implementer projects true status first hand?

616. How will the ISO IEC 27001 Lead Implementer project manage expectations & meet needs and requirements?

617. Timeline and milestones?

618. Have process improvement efforts been completed before requirements efforts begin?

619. Are meeting objectives identified for each meeting?

620. What is this ISO IEC 27001 Lead Implementer project aiming to achieve?

621. Does the ISO IEC 27001 Lead Implementer project have a Quality Culture?

622. Have ISO IEC 27001 Lead Implementer project success criteria been defined?

623. Do people have the competencies to meet the strategic objectives?

624. How are superior performers differentiated from average performers?

2.30 Communications Management Plan: ISO IEC 27001 Lead Implementer

625. What approaches to you feel are the best ones to use?

626. Who will use or be affected by the result of a ISO IEC 27001 Lead Implementer project?

627. Are there too many who have an interest in some aspect of your work?

628. Where do team members get information?

629. What are the interrelationships?

630. Which team member will work with each stakeholder?

631. Are others needed?

632. How will the person responsible for executing the communication item be notified?

633. Do you then often overlook a key stakeholder or stakeholder group?

634. What does the stakeholder need from the team?

635. Can you think of other people who might have concerns or interests?

636. How Did the Term Stakeholder Originate?

637. What help do you and your team need from the stakeholder?

638. Who is the stakeholder?

639. Why Is Stakeholder Engagement Important?

640. What approaches do you use?

641. Will messages be directly related to the release strategy or phases of the ISO IEC 27001 Lead Implementer project?

642. Do you feel a register helps?

643. What to learn?

2.31 Risk Management Plan: ISO IEC 27001 Lead Implementer

644. My ISO IEC 27001 Lead Implementer project leader has suddenly left the company, what do I do?

645. What are IT-specific requirements?

646. What are some questions that should be addressed in a risk management plan?

647. User Involvement: Do I have the right users?

648. What are the chances the risk event will occur?

649. What did not work so well?

650. How can you fix it?

651. What is the likelihood that the organization would accept responsibility for the risk?

652. Anticipated volatility of the requirements?

653. Was an original risk assessment/risk management plan completed?

654. What are the chances the event will occur?

655. Is the necessary data being captured and is it complete and accurate?

656. How are Risk Analysis and Prioritization

Performed?

657. Are the required plans included, such as nonstructural flood risk management plans?

658. Methodology: How will risk management be performed on this ISO IEC 27001 Lead Implementer project?

659. Risk Probability and Impact: How will the probabilities and impacts of risk items be assessed?

660. Are requirements fully understood by the software engineering team and customers?

661. Financial risk -can the organization afford to undertake the ISO IEC 27001 Lead Implementer project?

662. Internal technical and management reviews?

2.32 Risk Register: ISO IEC 27001 Lead Implementer

663. How is a Community Risk Register created?

664. What are the main aims, objectives of the policy, strategy, or service and the intended outcomes?

665. What Should The Audit Role Be In Establishing a Risk Management Process?

666. What may happen or not go according to plan?

667. What action, if any, has been taken to respond to the risk?

668. Manageability – Have mitigations to the risk been identified?

669. Market risk -Will the new service or product be useful to the organization or marketable to others?

670. What is the reason for current performance gaps and do the risks and opportunities identified previously explain this?

671. What are our key risks/showstoppers and what is being done to manage them?

672. Assume the risk event or situation happens, what would the impact be?

673. What is a Community Risk Register?

674. Is further information required before making a decision?

675. What are you going to do to limit the ISO IEC 27001 Lead Implementer projects risk exposure due to the identified risks?

676. What can be done about it?

677. Schedule Impact/Severity Estimated Range (workdays) Assume the event happens, what is the potential impact?

678. Whats the appropriate level of risk management for this ISO IEC 27001 Lead Implementer project?

679. Preventative actions - planned actions to reduce the likelihood a risk will occur and/or reduce the seriousness should it occur. What should you do now?

680. People risk -Are people with appropriate skills available to help complete the ISO IEC 27001 Lead Implementer project?

681. Risk Documentation: What reporting formats and processes will be used for risk management activities?

682. How well are risks controlled?

2.33 Probability and Impact Assessment: ISO IEC 27001 Lead Implementer

683. What are the channels available for distribution to the customer?

684. Mitigation -how can you avoid the risk?

685. Are there new risks that mitigation strategies might introduce?

686. Is it necessary to deeply assess all ISO IEC 27001 Lead Implementer project risks?

687. What is the impact if the risk does occur?

688. Is the ISO IEC 27001 Lead Implementer project cutting across the entire organization?

689. What can you do about it?

690. What are the probabilities of chosen technologies being suitable for local conditions?

691. What are the current demands of the customer?

692. What would be the effect of slippage?

693. Do you have a mechanism for managing change?

694. Is the technology to be built new to your organization?

695. Is security a central objective?

696. What risks does the organization have if the ISO IEC 27001 Lead Implementer projects fail to meet deadline?

697. Is the customer technically sophisticated in the product area?

698. Monitoring of the overall ISO IEC 27001 Lead Implementer project status – are there any changes in the ISO IEC 27001 Lead Implementer project that can effect and cause new possible risks?

699. Which risks need to move on to Perform Quantitative Risk Analysis?

700. Are the risk data timely and relevant?

701. Are tool mentors available?

2.34 Probability and Impact Matrix: ISO IEC 27001 Lead Implementer

702. What will be the likely incidence of conflict with neighboring ISO IEC 27001 Lead Implementer projects?

703. What should be the gestation period for the ISO IEC 27001 Lead Implementer project with this technology?

704. What needs to be DONE?

705. To what extent is the chosen technology maturing?

706. How is the ISO IEC 27001 Lead Implementer project going to be managed?

707. Do you have a consistent repeatable process that is actually used?

708. How do risks change during the ISO IEC 27001 Lead Implementer projects life cycle?

709. Do end-users have realistic expectations?

710. Can the risk be avoided by choosing a different alternative?

711. Economic to take on the ISO IEC 27001 Lead Implementer project?

712. Can you handle the investment risk?

713. What should be done with non-critical risks?

714. Can the ISO IEC 27001 Lead Implementer project proceed without assuming the risk?

715. Does the customer have a solid idea of what is required?

716. What is the likelihood?

717. How do you analyse the risks in the different types of ISO IEC 27001 Lead Implementer projects?

718. Do you train all developers in the process?

2.35 Risk Data Sheet: ISO IEC 27001 Lead Implementer

719. How do you handle product safely?

720. Potential for Recurrence?

721. Whom do you serve (customers)?

722. What can YOU do?

723. How can hazards be reduced?

724. How reliable is the data source?

725. What is the chance that it will happen?

726. What actions can be taken to eliminate or remove risk?

727. What are the main threats to our existence?

728. What is the duration of infection (the length of time the host is infected with the organizm) in a normal healthy human host?

729. Will revised controls lead to tolerable risk levels?

730. Risk of What?

731. Is the data sufficiently specified in terms of the type of failure being analysed, and its frequency or probability?

732. What Do you Know?

733. Has a sensitivity analysis been carried out?

734. What if client refuses?

735. Do effective diagnostic tests exist?

736. Would you prefer an unknown or 70/30 chance?

737. What do people affected think about the need for, and practicality of preventive measures?

738. Has the most cost-effective solution been chosen?

2.36 Procurement Management Plan: ISO IEC 27001 Lead Implementer

739. Financial capacity; does the seller have, or can the seller reasonably be expected to obtain, the financial resources needed?

740. Are procurement deliverables arriving on time and to specification?

741. Has an organization readiness assessment been conducted?

742. Have all unresolved risks been documented?

743. Are change requests logged and managed?

744. Have all involved ISO IEC 27001 Lead Implementer project stakeholders and work groups committed to the ISO IEC 27001 Lead Implementer project?

745. Are estimating assumptions and constraints captured?

746. Are Vendor contract reports, reviews and visits conducted periodically?

747. Is there a formal process for updating the ISO IEC 27001 Lead Implementer project baseline?

748. How will multiple providers be managed?

749. Is there a procurement management plan in place?

750. Does the detailed ISO IEC 27001 Lead Implementer project plan identify individual responsibilities for the next 4–6 weeks?

751. Has a provision been made to reassess ISO IEC 27001 Lead Implementer project risks at various ISO IEC 27001 Lead Implementer project stages?

752. Was the scope definition used in task sequencing?

753. Were ISO IEC 27001 Lead Implementer project team members involved in detailed estimating and scheduling?

2.37 Source Selection Criteria: ISO IEC 27001 Lead Implementer

754. What are the most critical evaluation criteria that prove to be tiebreakers in the evaluation of proposals?

755. Do you prepare an independent cost estimate?

756. What documentation should be used to support the selection decision?

757. Do you ensure you evaluate what you asked for, not what you want to see or expect to see?

758. What should a Draft Request for Proposal (DRFP) include?

759. How should comments received in response to a RFP be handled?

760. Is the offeror pricing what is technically proposed?

761. What are the limitations on pre-competitive range communications?

762. What Source Selection software is your team using?

763. How do you encourage efficiency and consistency?

764. Have team members been adequately trained?

765. What will you use to capture evaluation and subsequent documentation?

766. When is it appropriate to issue a DRFP?

767. Do you have designated specific forms or worksheets?

768. What information may not be provided?

769. In Which phase of the Acquisition Process Cycle does source qualifications reside?

770. Who should attend debriefings?

771. Are discussions anticipated?

772. Can you make a cost/technical tradeoff?

773. Are Resultant Proposal Revisions Allowed?

2.38 Stakeholder Management Plan: ISO IEC 27001 Lead Implementer

774. Has the scope management document been updated and distributed to help prevent scope creep?

775. Are you meeting your customers expectations consistently?

776. Are updated ISO IEC 27001 Lead Implementer project time & resource estimates reasonable based on the current ISO IEC 27001 Lead Implementer project stage?

777. Were ISO IEC 27001 Lead Implementer project team members involved in detailed estimating and scheduling?

778. Was your organizations estimating methodology being used and followed?

779. Why would you develop a ISO IEC 27001 Lead Implementer project Business Plan?

780. What has to be purchased?

781. What is the process for purchases that arent acceptable (eg damaged goods)?

782. What potential impact does the stakeholder have on the ISO IEC 27001 Lead Implementer project?

783. Is the performance of the supplier to be rated

and documented?

784. Have all involved ISO IEC 27001 Lead Implementer project stakeholders and work groups committed to the ISO IEC 27001 Lead Implementer project?

785. Describe the process that will be used to design, develop, review, accept, distribute and change outputs. Will all outputs delivered by the ISO IEC 27001 Lead Implementer project follow the same process?

786. Are there checklists created to demine if all quality processes are followed?

787. Is the communication plan being followed?

788. What are the advantages and disadvantages of using external contracted resources?

789. Do you know what your customers expectations are regarding this process?

790. What are the criteria for selecting other suppliers, including subcontractors?

2.39 Change Management Plan: ISO IEC 27001 Lead Implementer

791. What are the key change management success metrics?

792. Does this change represent a completely new process for the organization, or a different application of an existing process?

793. Who will be the change levers?

794. What provokes Organizational Change?

795. Identify the risk and assess the significance and likelihood of it occurring and plan the contingency What risks may occur upfront?

796. How will the stakeholders share information and transfer knowledge?

797. What change processes have you experienced in your organization in the last 2 years?

798. How can you best frame the message so that it addresses the audiences interests?

799. Is there a need for new relationships to be built?

800. Where will the funds come from?

801. What prerequisite knowledge do these groups need?

802. Clearly articulate the overall business benefits of the ISO IEC 27001 Lead Implementer project -why are you doing this now?

803. Who might present the most resistance?

804. Is there a software application relevant to this deliverable?

805. Who might be able to help you the most?

806. Readiness -What is a successful end state?

807. Who is responsible for which tasks?

808. What method and medium would you use to announce a message?

809. Who should be involved in developing a change management strategy?

810. Have the systems been configured and tested?

3.0 Executing Process Group: ISO IEC 27001 Lead Implementer

811. Do the products created live up to the necessary quality?

812. Have operating capacities been created and/or reinforced in partners?

813. What Business Situation Is Being Addressed?

814. How can you use Microsoft ISO IEC 27001 Lead Implementer project and Excel to assist in ISO IEC 27001 Lead Implementer project risk management?

815. Contingency planning. If a risk event occurs, what will you do?

816. What type of people would you want on your team?

817. On which process should team members spend the most time?

818. Is the ISO IEC 27001 Lead Implementer project making progress in helping to achieve the set results?

819. What are the typical ISO IEC 27001 Lead Implementer project management skills?

820. How well defined and documented were the ISO IEC 27001 Lead Implementer project management processes you chose to use?

821. Is activity definition the first process involved in ISO IEC 27001 Lead Implementer project time management?

822. What is involved in the solicitation process?

823. Is the schedule for the set products being met?

824. What is the product of your ISO IEC 27001 Lead Implementer project?

825. How can your organization use a weighted decision matrix to evaluate proposals as part of source selection?

826. What were things that you need to improve?

827. When will the ISO IEC 27001 Lead Implementer project be done?

828. How does a ISO IEC 27001 Lead Implementer project life cycle differ from a product life cycle?

829. What type of information goes in the quality assurance plan?

830. How well did the chosen processes fit the needs of the ISO IEC 27001 Lead Implementer project?

3.1 Team Member Status Report: ISO IEC 27001 Lead Implementer

831. Will the staff do training or is that done by a third party?

832. Are the products of the organization's ISO IEC 27001 Lead Implementer projects meeting their customer's objectives?

833. What specific interest groups do you have in place?

834. Why is it to be done?

835. How does this product, good, or service meet the needs of the ISO IEC 27001 Lead Implementer project and the organization as a whole?

836. How can you make it practical?

837. Are the organization's ISO IEC 27001 Lead Implementer projects more successful over time?

838. What is to be done?

839. Is there evidence that staff is taking a more professional approach toward management of the organizations ISO IEC 27001 Lead Implementer projects?

840. Does every department have to have a ISO IEC 27001 Lead Implementer project Manager on staff?

841. How much risk is involved?

842. When a teams productivity and success depend on collaboration and the efficient flow of information, what generally fails them?

843. The problem with Reward & Recognition Programs is that the truly deserving people all too often get left out. How can you make it practical?

844. Does the organization have the means (staff, money, contract, etc.) to produce or to acquire the product, good, or service?

845. How will Resource Planning be done?

846. Does the product, good, or service already exist within the organization?

847. Do you have an Enterprise ISO IEC 27001 Lead Implementer project Management Office (EPMO)?

848. Are the attitudes of staff regarding ISO IEC 27001 Lead Implementer project work improving?

849. How it is to be done?

3.2 Change Request: ISO IEC 27001 Lead Implementer

850. Has the change been highlighted and documented in the CSCI?

851. Can you answer what happened, who did it, when did it happen, and what else will be affected?

852. How many lines of code must be changed to implement the change?

853. What has an inspector to inspect and to check?

854. What type of changes does change control take into account?

855. Why were my requested changes rejected or not made?

856. Should a more thorough impact analysis be conducted?

857. What is the relationship between requirements attributes and attributes like complexity and size?

858. Will this change conflict with other requirements changes (e.g., lead to conflicting operational scenarios)?

859. Are there requirements attributes that are strongly related to the occurrence of defects and failures?

860. What mechanism is used to appraise others of changes that are made?

861. What should be regulated in a change control operating instruction?

862. What are the basic mechanics of the Change Advisory Board (CAB)?

863. What Can Be Filed?

864. How are the measures for carrying out the change established?

865. What kind of information about the change request needs to be captured?

866. How can you ensure that changes have been made properly?

867. Has your address changed?

868. How well do experienced software developers predict software change?

869. Have SCM procedures for noting the change, recording it, and reporting it been followed?

3.3 Change Log: ISO IEC 27001 Lead Implementer

870. Is the submitted change a new change or a modification of a previously approved change?

871. Is the requested change request a result of changes in other ISO IEC 27001 Lead Implementer project(s)?

872. Is this a mandatory replacement?

873. Will the ISO IEC 27001 Lead Implementer project fail if the change request is not executed?

874. How does this change affect the timeline of the schedule?

875. When was the request submitted?

876. How does this relate to the standards developed for specific business processes?

877. Do the described changes impact on the integrity or security of the system?

878. Is the change backward compatible without limitations?

879. Is the change request within ISO IEC 27001 Lead Implementer project scope?

880. Is the change request open, closed or pending?

881. Who initiated the change request?

882. When was the request approved?

883. Does the suggested change request seem to represent a necessary enhancement to the product?

884. How does this change affect scope?

3.4 Decision Log: ISO IEC 27001 Lead Implementer

885. What makes you different or better than others companies selling the same thing?

886. Is your opponent open to a non-traditional workflow, or will it likely challenge anything you do?

887. How does an increasing emphasis on cost containment influence the strategies and tactics used?

888. How does provision of information, both in terms of content and presentation, influence acceptance of alternative strategies?

889. Behaviors; what are guidelines that the team has identified that will assist them with getting the most out of their team meetings?

890. Meeting purpose; why does this team meet?

891. What was the rationale for the decision?

892. Who will be given a copy of this document and where will it be kept?

893. Decision-making process; how will the team make decisions?

894. How do you define success?

895. With whom was the decision shared or discussed?

896. So, what is the line where eDiscovery ends and document review begins?

897. What alternatives/risks were considered?

898. Who is the decisionmaker?

899. How effective is maintaining the log at facilitating organizational learning?

900. How does the use a Decision Support System influence the strategies/tactics or costs?

901. Is everything working as expected?

902. At what point in time does loss become unacceptable?

903. Which variables make a critical difference?

904. How consolidated and comprehensive a story can we tell by capturing currently available incident data in a central location and through a log of key decisions during an incident?

3.5 Quality Audit: ISO IEC 27001 Lead Implementer

905. What is your organizations greatest strength?

906. How does the organization know that its risk management system is appropriately effective and constructive?

907. Are people allowed to contribute ideas?

908. How does the organization know that the support for its staff is appropriately effective and constructive?

909. Are storage areas and reconditioning operations designed to prevent mix-ups and assure orderly handling of both the distressed and reconditioned devices?

910. How is the Strategic Plan (and other plans) reviewed and revised?

911. Does the audit organization have experience in performing the required work for entities of your type and size?

912. How does the organization know that its Mission, Vision and Values Statements are appropriate and effectively guiding the organization?

913. What has changed/improved as a result of the review processes?

914. How does the organization know that it is maintaining a conducive staff climate?

915. How does the organization know that its security arrangements are appropriately effective and constructive?

916. How does the organization know that it is effectively and constructively guiding staff through to timely completion of their tasks?

917. Are there appropriate indicators for monitoring the effectiveness and efficiency of processes?

918. What does an analysis of an organizations staff profile suggest in terms of its planning, and how is this being addressed?

919. Does the suppliers quality system have a written procedure for corrective action when a defect occurs?

920. How does the organization know that its industry and community engagement planning and management systems are appropriately effective and constructive in enabling relationships with key stakeholder groups?

921. How does your organization ensure that equipment is appropriately maintained and producing valid results?

922. How does the organization know that its research programs are appropriately effective and constructive?

923. How does the organization know that its research planning and management systems are appropriately effective and constructive in enabling quality research outcomes?

924. What data about organizational performance is routinely collected and reported?

3.6 Team Directory: ISO IEC 27001 Lead Implementer

925. What are you going to deliver or accomplish?

926. Does a ISO IEC 27001 Lead Implementer project team directory list all resources assigned to the ISO IEC 27001 Lead Implementer project?

927. Process Decisions: Are contractors adequately prosecuting the work?

928. Is construction on schedule?

929. Who is the Sponsor?

930. Have you decided when to celebrate the ISO IEC 27001 Lead Implementer projects completion date?

931. Where should the information be distributed?

932. How will the team handle changes?

933. Process Decisions: Which organizational elements and which individuals will be assigned management functions?

934. Where will the product be used and/or delivered or built when appropriate?

935. Process Decisions: Do job conditions warrant additional actions to collect job information and document on-site activity?

936. When will you produce deliverables?

937. Process Decisions: Do invoice amounts match accepted work in place?

938. Process Decisions: Are all start-up, turn over and close out requirements of the contract satisfied?

939. How do unidentified risks impact the outcome of the ISO IEC 27001 Lead Implementer project?

940. Who will write the meeting minutes and distribute?

941. Who are the Team Members?

942. When does information need to be distributed?

943. Process Decisions: Are all issues being addressed to the satisfaction of both parties within approximately 30 days from the time the issue is identified?

3.7 Team Operating Agreement: ISO IEC 27001 Lead Implementer

944. What is the number of cases currently teamed?

945. Why does the organization want to participate in teaming?

946. Has the appropriate access to relevant data and analysis capability been granted?

947. What resources can be provided for the team in terms of equipment, space, time for training, protected time and space for meetings, and travel allowances?

948. What are some potential sources of conflict among team members?

949. What is Teaming?

950. Do you leverage technology engagement tools group chat, polls, screen sharing, etc.?

951. What is a Virtual Team?

952. Must your members collaborate successfully to complete ISO IEC 27001 Lead Implementer projects?

953. What is the anticipated procedure (recruitment, solicitation of volunteers, or assignment) for selecting team members?

954. Did you draft the meeting agenda?

955. Have you established procedures that team members can follow to work effectively together, such as a team operating agreement?

956. How do you want to be thought of and known within the organization?

957. Do you send out the agenda and meeting materials in advance?

958. Resource Allocation: How will individual team members account for their time and expenses, and how will this be allocated in the team budget?

959. The method to be used in the decision making process; Will it be consensus, majority rule, or the supervisor having the final say?

960. Reimbursements: How will the team members be reimbursed for expenses and time commitments?

961. To whom do you deliver our services?

962. Do you record meetings for those unable to attend?

963. Are team roles clearly defined and accepted?

3.8 Team Performance Assessment: ISO IEC 27001 Lead Implementer

964. When a reviewer complains about method variance, what is the essence of the complaint?

965. Do friends perform better than acquaintances?

966. To what degree do team members feel that the purpose of the team is important, if not exciting?

967. To what degree can the team ensure that all members are individually and jointly accountable for the teams purpose, goals, approach, and work-products?

968. How do you encourage members to learn from each other?

969. To what degree are the relative importance and priority of the goals clear to all team members?

970. To what degree are staff involved as partners in the improvement process?

971. If you are worried about method variance before you collect data, what sort of design elements might you include to reduce or eliminate the threat of method variance?

972. How hard do you try to make a good selection?

973. To what degree do team members frequently

explore the teams purpose and its implications?

974. To what degree do team members understand one anothers roles and skills?

975. Do you give group members authority to make at least some important decisions?

976. To what degree will new and supplemental skills be introduced as the need is recognized?

977. To what degree do team members articulate the teams work approach?

978. Individual task proficiency and team process behavior: Whats important for team functioning?

979. To what degree are the teams goals and objectives clear, simple, and measurable?

980. To what degree are the skill areas critical to team performance present?

981. To what degree do all members feel responsible for all agreed-upon measures?

982. To what degree does the team possess adequate membership to achieve its ends?

3.9 Team Member Performance Assessment: ISO IEC 27001 Lead Implementer

983. What is used as a basis for instructional decisions?

984. Why were these selected?

985. To what degree are the goals ambitious?

986. What is collaboration?

987. What are the key duties or tasks of the Ratee?

988. How was the determination made for which training platforms would be used (i.e., media selection)?

989. What were the challenges that resulted for training and assessment?

990. In what areas would you like to concentrate your knowledge and resources?

991. To what degree do members articulate the goals beyond the team membership?

992. How will they be formed?

993. Are assessment validation activities performed?

994. What is the Business Management Oversight

Process?

995. To what degree is there a sense that only the team can succeed?

996. Why do performance reviews?

997. Is There Reluctance to Join a Team?

998. Is it clear how goals will be accomplished?

999. Is it critical or vital to the job?

3.10 Issue Log: ISO IEC 27001 Lead Implementer

1000. How is this initiative related to other portfolios, programs, or ISO IEC 27001 Lead Implementer projects?

1001. What is a change?

1002. In your work, how much time is spent on stakeholder identification?

1003. Are you constantly rushing from meeting to meeting?

1004. What is the stakeholders political influence?

1005. What effort will a change need?

1006. What are the typical contents?

1007. Are the ISO IEC 27001 Lead Implementer project Issues uniquely identified, including to which product they refer?

1008. Do you often overlook a key stakeholder or stakeholder group?

1009. What help do you and your team need from the stakeholders?

1010. How Do you Manage Communications?

1011. How much time does it take to do it?

1012. Who is involved as you identify stakeholders?

1013. Who needs to know and how much?

1014. Are the stakeholders getting the information they need, are they consulted, are their concerns addressed?

1015. What would have to change?

1016. Which stakeholders are thought leaders, influences, or early adopters?

4.0 Monitoring and Controlling Process Group: ISO IEC 27001 Lead Implementer

1017. What is the timeline?

1018. How well did the team follow the chosen processes?

1019. Is there sufficient time allotted between the general system design and the detailed system design phases?

1020. Were sponsors and decision makers available when needed outside regularly scheduled meetings?

1021. Do the partners have sufficient financial capacity to keep up the benefits produced by the programme?

1022. What areas does the group agree are the biggest success on the ISO IEC 27001 Lead Implementer project?

1023. Are there areas that need improvement?

1024. Is there sufficient funding available for this?

1025. What is the timeline for the ISO IEC 27001 Lead Implementer project?

1026. But Did It Work?

1027. Is progress on outcomes due to your program?

1028. How Well Did You Do?

1029. Did you implement the program as designed?

1030. How is Agile Portfolio Management done?

1031. Does the solution fit in with organizations technical architectural requirements?

1032. What kinds of things in particular are you looking for data on?

1033. How many more potential communications channels were introduced by the discovery of the new stakeholders?

4.1 Project Performance Report: ISO IEC 27001 Lead Implementer

1034. To what degree are the structures of the formal organization consistent with the behaviors in the informal organization?

1035. To what degree can team members vigorously define the team's purpose in discussions with others who are not part of the functioning team?

1036. What is the degree to which rules govern information exchange between individuals within the organization?

1037. To what degree will team members, individually and collectively, commit time to help themselves and others learn and develop skills?

1038. To what degree does the team's purpose contain themes that are particularly meaningful and memorable?

1039. To what degree does the team's work approach provide opportunity for members to engage in open interaction?

1040. To what degree does the team's work approach provide opportunity for members to engage in results-based evaluation?

1041. To what degree is the team cognizant of small wins to be celebrated along the way?

1042. To what degree are the members clear on what they are individually responsible for and what they are jointly responsible for?

1043. To what degree will the approach capitalize on and enhance the skills of all team members in a manner that takes into consideration other demands on members of the team?

1044. To what degree does the informal organization make use of individual resources and meet individual needs?

1045. To what degree does the team's purpose constitute a broader, deeper aspiration than just accomplishing short-term goals?

1046. To what degree are the demands of the task compatible with and converge with the mission and functions of the formal organization?

1047. How will procurement be coordinated with other ISO IEC 27001 Lead Implementer project aspects, such as scheduling and performance reporting?

1048. To what degree can team members frequently and easily communicate with one another?

1049. What degree are the relative importance and priority of the goals clear to all team members?

1050. To what degree does the team's work approach provide opportunity for members to engage in fact-based problem solving?

4.2 Variance Analysis: ISO IEC 27001 Lead Implementer

1051. What causes selling price variance?

1052. Are meaningful indicators identified for use in measuring the status of cost and schedule performance?

1053. Are there quarterly budgets with quarterly performance comparisons?

1054. Budget versus Actual. How does the monthly budget compare to actual experience?

1055. What is the incurrence of actual indirect costs in excess of budgets, by element of expense?

1056. Other relevant issues of Variance Analysis -selling price or gross margin?

1057. Do the rates and prices remain constant throughout the year?

1058. Is the entire contract planned in time-phased control accounts to the extent practicable?

1059. Does the contractors system identify work accomplishment against the schedule plan?

1060. Is the market likely to continue to grow at this rate next year?

1061. Are there changes in the overhead pool and/or organization structures?

1062. How have the setting and use of standards changed over time?

1063. Is there a logical explanation for any variance?

1064. How does the monthly budget compare to the actual experience?

1065. What is your organizations rationale for sharing expenses and services between business segments?

1066. Are authorized changes being incorporated in a timely manner?

1067. How are material, labor, and overhead variances calculated and recorded?

1068. What is the actual cost of work performed?

1069. Who is generally responsible for monitoring and taking action on variances?

4.3 Earned Value Status: ISO IEC 27001 Lead Implementer

1070. Where is Evidence-based Earned Value in your organization reported?

1071. How does this compare with other ISO IEC 27001 Lead Implementer projects?

1072. Where are your problem areas?

1073. What is the unit of forecast value?

1074. When is it going to finish?

1075. If earned value management (EVM) is so good in determining the true status of a ISO IEC 27001 Lead Implementer project and ISO IEC 27001 Lead Implementer project its completion, why is it that hardly any one uses it in information systems related ISO IEC 27001 Lead Implementer projects?

1076. Earned Value can be used in almost any ISO IEC 27001 Lead Implementer project situation and in almost any ISO IEC 27001 Lead Implementer project environment. It may be used on large ISO IEC 27001 Lead Implementer projects, medium sized ISO IEC 27001 Lead Implementer projects, tiny ISO IEC 27001 Lead Implementer projects (in cut-down form), complex and simple ISO IEC 27001 Lead Implementer projects and in any market sector. Some people, of course, know all about earned value, they have used it for years - but perhaps not as effectively as they could have?

1077. Verification is a process of ensuring that the developed system satisfies the stakeholders agreements and specifications; Are you building the product right? What do you verify?

1078. Are you hitting your ISO IEC 27001 Lead Implementer projects targets?

1079. How much is it going to cost by the finish?

1080. Validation is a process of ensuring that the developed system will actually achieve the stakeholders desired outcomes; Are you building the right product? What do you validate?

4.4 Risk Audit: ISO IEC 27001 Lead Implementer

1081. What risk does not having unique identification present?

1082. Is all expenditure authorised through an identified process?

1083. What effect would a better risk management program have had?

1084. How are risk appetites expressed?

1085. What are the Internal Controls ?

1086. Strategic business risk audit methodologies; are these an attempt to sell other services, and is management becoming the client of the audit rather than the shareholder?

1087. What is the effect of globalisation; is business becoming too complex and can the auditor rely on auditing standards?

1088. Can analytical tests provide evidence that is as strong as evidence from traditional substantive tests?

1089. Do industry specialists and business risk auditors enhance audit reporting accuracy?

1090. Is Risk an management agenda item?

1091. Are your rules, by-laws and practices non-discriminatory?

1092. Is the number of people on the ISO IEC 27001 Lead Implementer project team adequate to do the job?

1093. Is there a screening process that will ensure all participants have the fitness and skills required to safely participate?

1094. What programmatic and Fiscal information is being collected and analyzed?

1095. Whence the business risk audit?

1096. Do you have financial policies and procedures in place to guide officers of the organization/treasurer/general members?

1097. Will an appropriate standard of care be applied to all involved?

1098. For paid staff, does your organization comply with the minimum conditions for employment and/or the applicable modern award?

4.5 Contractor Status Report: ISO IEC 27001 Lead Implementer

1099. What was the overall budget or estimated cost?

1100. Describe how often regular updates are made to the proposed solution. Are these regular updates included in the standard maintenance plan?

1101. What process manages the contracts?

1102. How long have you been using the services?

1103. What are the minimum and optimal bandwidth requirements for the proposed soluiton?

1104. Who can list a ISO IEC 27001 Lead Implementer project as company experience, the company or a previous employee of the company?

1105. What was the final actual cost?

1106. What was the budget or estimated cost for your companys services?

1107. How does the proposed individual meet each requirement?

1108. If applicable; describe your standard schedule for new software version releases. Are new software version releases included in the standard maintenance plan?

1109. What was the actual budget or estimated cost for your companys services?

1110. Are there contractual transfer concerns?

1111. What is the average response time for answering a support call?

1112. How is Risk Transferred?

4.6 Formal Acceptance: ISO IEC 27001 Lead Implementer

1113. What features, practices, and processes proved to be strengths or weaknesses?

1114. What are the requirements against which to test, Who will execute?

1115. Is formal acceptance of the ISO IEC 27001 Lead Implementer project product documented and distributed?

1116. Did the ISO IEC 27001 Lead Implementer project manager and team act in a professional and ethical manner?

1117. What function(s) does it fill or meet?

1118. Did the ISO IEC 27001 Lead Implementer project achieve its MOV?

1119. Was the client satisfied with the ISO IEC 27001 Lead Implementer project results?

1120. Have all comments been addressed?

1121. Who would use it?

1122. What lessons were learned about your ISO IEC 27001 Lead Implementer project management methodology?

1123. Does it do what ISO IEC 27001 Lead Implementer project team said it would?

1124. Was the ISO IEC 27001 Lead Implementer project goal achieved?

1125. Do you perform formal acceptance or burn-in tests?

1126. How well did the team follow the methodology?

1127. Was the ISO IEC 27001 Lead Implementer project managed well?

1128. Do you buy-in installation services?

1129. How does your team plan to obtain formal acceptance on your ISO IEC 27001 Lead Implementer project?

1130. Was the ISO IEC 27001 Lead Implementer project work done on time, within budget, and according to specification?

1131. Do you buy pre-configured systems or build your own configuration?

1132. General estimate of the costs and times to complete the ISO IEC 27001 Lead Implementer project?

5.0 Closing Process Group: ISO IEC 27001 Lead Implementer

1133. Is the ISO IEC 27001 Lead Implementer project Funded?

1134. Did the ISO IEC 27001 Lead Implementer project team have enough people to execute the ISO IEC 27001 Lead Implementer project plan?

1135. What could be done to improve the process?

1136. What were things that you did very well and want to do the same again on the next ISO IEC 27001 Lead Implementer project?

1137. Just how important is your work to the overall success of the ISO IEC 27001 Lead Implementer project?

1138. Specific - Is the objective clear in terms of what, how, when, and where the situation will be changed?

1139. What is the amount of funding and what ISO IEC 27001 Lead Implementer project phases are funded?

1140. Is this a follow-on to a previous ISO IEC 27001 Lead Implementer project?

1141. Did the ISO IEC 27001 Lead Implementer project team have the right skills?

1142. Did you do what you said you were going to do?

1143. What was learned?

1144. Did the delivered product meet the specified requirements and goals of the ISO IEC 27001 Lead Implementer project?

1145. Who are the ISO IEC 27001 Lead Implementer project stakeholders?

1146. Is there a clear cause and effect between the activity and the lesson learned?

1147. Was the schedule met?

5.1 Procurement Audit: ISO IEC 27001 Lead Implementer

1148. Are all initial purchase contracts made by the purchasing organization?

1149. Has it been determined how large a portion of the procurement portfolio should be managed by the procurement function/unit and how large a portion that should be managed locally?

1150. Are there procedures for trade-in arrangements?

1151. Are criteria and sub-criteria set suitable to identify the tender that offers best value for money?

1152. Are regulations and protective measures in place to avoid corruption?

1153. Is there a procedure to summarize bids and select a vendor?

1154. Are order quantities, deliveries and payment levels under the contract monitored by an appropriate official?

1155. Is the weighting set coherent, convincing and leaving little scope for arbitrary and random evaluation and ranking?

1156. Are review meetings organized during contract execution and do they meet demand?

1157. Does the procurement unit have sound commercial awareness and knowledge of suppliers and the market?

1158. Were additional deliveries a partial replacement for normal supplies or installations or an extension of existing supplies or installations?

1159. Is there no evidence that the consultants participating in the ISO IEC 27001 Lead Implementer project design released information to contractors competing for the prime contract?

1160. Was the organization specific about the nature and scope of the performance before launching the procurement process?

1161. Is there no evidence of unauthorized release of information or seemingly unnecessary contacts with bidders personnel during the evaluation and negotiation processes?

1162. Are the official minutes written in a clear and concise manner?

1163. Were any additional works or deliveries admissible without the need for a new procurement procedure?

1164. Relevance of the contract to the Internal Market?

1165. Could bidders learn all relevant information straight from the tender documents?

1166. Where funding is being arranged by borrowings, do these have the necessary approval and legal authority?

1167. In case of decisions not to conclude a procurement or award a contract, were tenderers informed in writing and on a timely basis of those decisions and their grounds?

5.2 Contract Close-Out: ISO IEC 27001 Lead Implementer

1168. How/When Used ?

1169. How is the contracting office notified of the automatic contract close-out?

1170. Have all contracts been closed?

1171. Was the contract type appropriate?

1172. A change in circumstances?

1173. How does it work?

1174. Have all contracts been completed?

1175. A change in attitude or behavior?

1176. Parties: Authorized?

1177. Are the signers the authorized officials?

1178. Have all contract records been included in the ISO IEC 27001 Lead Implementer project archives?

1179. Why Outsource?

1180. A change in knowledge?

1181. What happens to the recipient of services?

1182. Has each contract been audited to verify acceptance and delivery?

1183. Was the contract sufficiently clear so as not to result in numerous disputes and misunderstandings?

1184. Parties: Who is Involved?

1185. Have all acceptance criteria been met prior to final payment to contractors?

1186. What is Capture Management?

1187. Was the contract complete without requiring numerous changes and revisions?

5.3 Project or Phase Close-Out: ISO IEC 27001 Lead Implementer

1188. In addition to assessing whether the ISO IEC 27001 Lead Implementer project was successful, it is equally critical to analyze why it was or was not fully successful. Are you including this?

1189. When and how were information needs best met?

1190. What is in it for you?

1191. In preparing the Lessons Learned report, should it reflect a consensus viewpoint, or should the report reflect the different individual viewpoints?

1192. What were the actual outcomes?

1193. What was the preferred delivery mechanism?

1194. Is the lesson based on actual ISO IEC 27001 Lead Implementer project experience rather than on independent research?

1195. Who is Responsible for Award Close-out?

1196. Have business partners been involved extensively, and what data was required for them?

1197. What benefits or impacts does the stakeholder group expect to obtain as a result of the ISO IEC 27001 Lead Implementer project?

1198. What is a Risk?

1199. What hierarchical authority does the stakeholder have in the organization?

1200. Did the ISO IEC 27001 Lead Implementer project management methodology work?

1201. Planned Completion Date?

1202. What are the mandatory communication needs for each stakeholder?

1203. Does the lesson educate others to improve performance?

1204. What is the information level of detail required for each stakeholder?

1205. What information is each stakeholder group interested in?

1206. Who controlled key decisions that were made?

1207. Who are the ISO IEC 27001 Lead Implementer project stakeholders and what are their roles and involvement?

5.4 Lessons Learned: ISO IEC 27001 Lead Implementer

1208. Was the necessary hardware, software, accommodation etc available?

1209. What was helpful to know when planning the deployment?

1210. How many government and contractor personnel are authorized for the ISO IEC 27001 Lead Implementer project?

1211. How well did the ISO IEC 27001 Lead Implementer project Manager respond to questions or comments related to the ISO IEC 27001 Lead Implementer project?

1212. Is your organization willing to expose problems or mistakes for the betterment of the collective whole, and can you do this in a way that does not intimidate employees or workers?

1213. Were quality procedures built into the ISO IEC 27001 Lead Implementer project?

1214. How effective were ISO IEC 27001 Lead Implementer project audits?

1215. What is your overall assessment of the outcome of this ISO IEC 27001 Lead Implementer project?

1216. Did the ISO IEC 27001 Lead Implementer project

change significantly?

1217. How closely did deliverables match what was defined within the ISO IEC 27001 Lead Implementer project Scope?

1218. How effective was the training you received in preparation for the use of the product/service?

1219. Overall, how effective were the efforts to prepare you and your organization for the impact of the product/service of the ISO IEC 27001 Lead Implementer project?

1220. What worked well or did not work well, either for this ISO IEC 27001 Lead Implementer project or for the ISO IEC 27001 Lead Implementer project team?

1221. What things surprised you on the ISO IEC 27001 Lead Implementer project that were not in the plan?

1222. What was the geopolitical history during the origin of the organization and at the time of task input?

1223. What on the ISO IEC 27001 Lead Implementer project worked well and was effective in the delivery of the product?

1224. How useful was the format and content of the ISO IEC 27001 Lead Implementer project Status Report to you?

1225. How effectively and consistently was sponsorship for the ISO IEC 27001 Lead Implementer project conveyed?

1226. Did the delivered product meet the specified requirements and goals of the ISO IEC 27001 Lead Implementer project?

Index

255